WILL JESUS KNOW YOU?

Will Jesus Know You?

The Blueprint to mold your heart to the Heart of the Father!

Jason Butler

PALMETTO
P U B L I S H I N G
Charleston, SC
www.PalmettoPublishing.com

Copyright © 2024 by Jason Butler

All rights reserved including the right to reproduce this book or portions thereof in any form whatsoever. This book or parts thereof may not be reproduced in any form, stored in a retrieval system, or transmitted in any form by any means – electronic, mechanical, photocopy, recording, or otherwise – without prior written permission of the publisher, except as provided by United States of America copyright law.

Unless otherwise noted, all scripture quotations are taken from the Holy Bible, New Living Translation, copyright ©1996, 2004, 2015 by Tyndale House Foundation. Used by permission of Tyndale House Publishers, Carol Stream, Illinois 60188. All rights reserved.

Scripture quotations marked (NIV) are taken from the Holy Bible, New International Version®, NIV®. Copyright © 1973, 1978, 1984, 2011 by Biblica, Inc.™ Used by permission of Zondervan. All rights reserved worldwide. www.zondervan.com The "NIV" and "New International Version" are trademarks registered in the United States Patent and Trademark Office by Biblica, Inc.™

Scripture taken from the New King James Version®. Copyright © 1982 by Thomas Nelson. Used by permission. All rights reserved.

Requests for information should be addressed to: followhimwithus@gmail.com

To schedule Jason Butler to speak to your group, church, conference, or event, please send an email to followhimwithus@gmail.com. Please include your contact information, including your preferred method of contact (phone, email, text, letter, etc.).

Cover Design by Lamar Printing, LLC 329 Sanderson St, Alcoa, TN 37701
(865) 984-9148
Editing by Follow Him With Us Publishing

Hardcover ISBN – 979-8-9900024-1-8
Paperback ISBN – 979-8-9900024-4-9

Library of Congress Control Number: 2024903288

Contents

Introduction		ix
	A little bit of housekeeping…	xi
1	**Let's start at the beginning**	**1**
	In the beginning….	1
	To know someone….	3
	Why is that sermon important??	5
	Even the demons believe and know Jesus….	5
	Is it enough to know???	6
	Questions and Application for Chapter 1	8
	Prayer	8
2	**Matthew, the disciple**	**9**
	Why Matthew?	9
	The Will of the Father…	11
	The Lineage of Jesus….	11
	True Intimacy…	13
	This is personal for me…	15
	Questions and Application for Chapter 2	17
	Prayer	17
3	**The Sermon on the Mount**	**18**
	The heart behind the actions…	18
	The Blessings….	20
	Matthew 5:3-12 (NLT)	22
	The world versus The Kingdom…	22
	Questions and Application for Chapter 3	25
	Prayer	25
4	**Understanding the "Blessings"**	**26**
	The poor…the poor in spirit…(Matthew 5:3)	26
	Those who mourn….	
	God blesses those who mourn…(Matthew 5:4)	29

	Those who are humble....	
	God blesses those who are humble...(Matthew 5:5)	30
	Those who hunger and thirst for justice	
	or righteousness....will be satisfied...(Matthew 5:6)	32
	Those who are merciful	
	will be shown mercy...(Matthew 5:7)	33
	Those with pure hearts will see God...(Matthew 5:8)	34
	Those who work for Peace...(Matthew 5:9)	36
	Those who are persecuted	
	for doing right...(Matthew 5:10)	37
	Those who are mocked, lied about,	
	and persecuted for doing right...(Matthew 5:11-12)	38
	Summing up the blessings...	39
	Questions and Application for Chapter 4	41
	Prayer	42
5	**Salt and Light**	**43**
	Are you salty?	43
	Fertilizer? The Dung Pile?	46
	Pass me MORE salt please...	47
	Do you have flavor or are you bland?	48
	Are you a bright light?	48
	It's up to you how bright you want to be....	49
	Time to evaluate.....	52
	Good list vs the bad list.....	54
	Galatians 5 verses 19-23:	54
	Questions and Application for Chapter 5	57
	Prayer	57
6	**The Law...**	**59**
	Don't misunderstand...	59
	Jesus came to accomplish or fulfill	62
	Fenced in....	63
	Till heaven and earth disappear...	65
	Man, I hate hypocrisy...	65
	Religion...Greazy Grace...	66
	Details matter...	67
	A jot or a tittle...	68
	Solomon changed a lot with a jot!	70
	The least in the kingdom....	71
	The minimums....	72

	Let's give an example about adoption…	74
	At least do the minimums!	75
	A warning….	76
	Questions and Application for Chapter 6	78
	Prayer	78
7	**oh…no…Jesus actually makes it harder… as He fully preaches it…**	**79**
	Anger is murder…	79
	Learning to take the thought captive…	81
	The fear pendulum…	85
	Most fear and worry is irrational…	90
	Sound mind…	92
	What about the "Good fear"???	93
	Questions and Application for Chapter 7	95
	Prayer	95
8	**still harder…**	**96**
	Lust is adultery…	96
	Lust from the beginning…	98
	Same lust today…	99
	Bounce your heart…	101
	Divorce…	102
	The big 3 things that ruin a marriage…	104
	Questions and Application for Chapter 8	107
	Prayer	107
9	**how we treat people matters…**	**108**
	Promises…	108
	Revenge…	112
	Love your enemies…	113
	This is sort of hard to live out…	115
	Questions and Application for Chapter 9	119
	Prayer	119
10	**are you just trying to look good for others to see???**	**120**
	Good deeds again…	120
	Giving to those in need…	122
	Giving for the wrong reason…	123
	Prayer…	124
	The "Jewish" Prayers…	127

	Finally…explaining the Lord's Prayer…	129
	Our Daily Bread…	133
	Ra ra…	133
	Giving credit where credit is due!	134
	Questions and Application for Chapter 10	135
	Prayer	135
11	**are you telling me that I have to forgive others???**	**136**
	It's conditional…	136
	Let go…	137
	Benefits of forgiveness…	139
	70x7…	141
	I can't forgive them…they are dead…	143
	Let's do this! I'm ready to forgive…	145
	Trust the process…	148
	What about you???	149
12	**you hungry yet???**	**150**
	When you fast…	150
	Everyone's question about fasting…	152
	The Daniel fast…	153
	Questions and Application for Chapter 12	155
	Prayer	155
13	**money and stuff…and worry…**	**156**
	Where are you storing your treasures…	156
	The American Dream…	159
	The Eternal Dream!	161
	Colossians 3:23 – great motto!	162
	One Master at a time…	162
	The Rich Young Ruler…	164
	How big is that needle?	165
	Do we really trust God?	166
	Seek the Kingdom first…	169
	Questions and Application for Chapter 13	171
	Prayer	171
14	**judging…**	**172**
	Can we judge? Should we judge?	172
	Hypocrisy…	175
	Don't cast your pearls to pigs…	176

	Paul has something to say about this too…	177
	Stringing pearls together…	178
	More Credit due!	182
	Questions and Application for Chapter 14	183
	Prayer	183
15	**More good info on prayer!**	**184**
	Is it ok to ask God for something more than once?	184
	Shameless persistence….	186
	Good gifts from a good Father!	186
	Questions and Application for Chapter 15	188
	Prayer	188
16	**The build up before the BIG VERSE!**	**189**
	The Golden Rule…	189
	The Narrow Gate…	191
	Only half will get in???	193
	Actions speak louder than words…	194
	Beware of the ole false prophet…	196
	Is this good or bad fruit?	201
	Ready for a true prophecy???	203
	Questions and Application for Chapter 16	205
	Prayer	205
17	**The grand finale!**	**206**
	The big verse!	206
	The sinner's prayer…	208
	Final instructions…	211
	Final Q&A	214
	Prayer	214

Introduction

As followers of Jesus, we often think that the most important thing that we can do in our lifetime is to make sure that we "know Jesus", right? Also, we want to make sure that others "know Jesus". Shouldn't that be our goal? Shouldn't our goal be to make sure that we know Jesus and to make sure that others we encounter know Jesus? That is certainly a great goal, but is it the most important question that we can ask? Is there a better question, a deeper question, that we should ask? I believe there is a better question that we need to start asking – WILL JESUS KNOW ME? WILL JESUS KNOW YOU?

"Do you know Jesus?" is a great starting place, but Jesus makes it clear in Matthew 7 verses 21-23 that not everyone who knows Him will enter the Kingdom of Heaven. In verse 23, He says "I never knew you. Get away from Me….". Those are words that I can't imagine hearing on the day I meet Jesus for judgement. As believers in Jesus, we look forward to the day that we will meet Him. We look forward to the time that we will spend in paradise with Him, for eternity. But, what if we get to that day, and hear the words "I never knew you"?

"Knowing Jesus" is a great starting place, but being "known by Jesus" should be the ultimate goal for each of us as Christ followers, and it should be the ultimate goal for all those that we tell and teach about Jesus. When we read that scripture in Matthew 7, it should ignite a desire within us to strive each day to be known by Jesus. We WANT to be known by Jesus on the day of judgement!

Many people are led to Jesus just by praying the "sinner's prayer", but then there is no life change. There is no discipleship. There is no repentance. I am concerned that there are many people on this Earth today that know Jesus, but aren't known by Him. At the other extreme, I think there are many people that are known by Jesus, but may be misled or lied to by our enemy, satan (the father of lies), to believe that they aren't known by Jesus.

So, I have a goal with this book. I have a goal for myself. I have a goal for my family. I have a goal for my church family. I have a goal for every reader that picks up this book. **First of all, I want to make sure that we know Jesus. Second, I want to make sure that we know what it means to be known BY Jesus. Finally, I want to make sure that we are secure in knowing that we are known by Jesus.**

We will tackle these questions by going directly to scripture. This will not be based on my opinions, nor will it be based on someone else's ideas or opinions. It will not be based on other written commentaries, nor will it be based on denominational influence. This will come 100% from reading the words of Jesus, given to us in the Bible.

Here's the good news for us as we start this journey. When Jesus says those words "I never knew you", He is near the end of the most famous sermon ever preached – the famed Sermon on the Mount. The good news is that Jesus has spent nearly 3 chapters in the book of Matthew telling us what it means to be known by Him. He gives us a blueprint so that we can be secure and confident in knowing that He'll know us!

We'll have to be careful to find middle ground as we explore this topic. We don't want to turn the Grace, given by Jesus, into something it never was, nor do we want to get lured down the path of trying to work our way into the Kingdom of Heaven. Scripture is clear that we are saved by the Grace of Jesus dying on the cross for our sins; but scripture is also clear that we are designed to do good works for Jesus because of that sacrifice He made for us. My goal and promise is to try and find this balance as we explore the greatest question a Christian can ever ask:

WILL JESUS KNOW ME?

A little bit of housekeeping...

At the end of each chapter, I will list out questions for self-reflection, and I will issue challenges for applying what you learn here. I will also list out a prayer for us to pray together. I don't want this book to only be more knowledge, or to only be a refresher of the knowledge you already have. I want this book to help scripture come alive for you in a way that you'll want to apply what you have learned or what you already knew!

You will notice that I work hard to capitalize God, Jesus, The Holy Spirit, and I work hard to capitalize any reference to Them (He, Him, etc.). I do that as a small way to keep the name of God Holy. He is set apart and holy, and it's a small way for me to honor Him. Likewise, I work hard to NOT capitalize the name of our enemy, satan. He will not be lifted up like Jesus will be, and I purposely remind you of that by not capitalizing his name.

I have poured my heart and soul into this book, sharing very vulnerable stories about my journey to be known. I would love to hear feedback from you. I would love to hear testimonies of God's redemption! I would love to hear how you have been challenged and made life changes, after reading God's word. I would love to help those that are still confused or still have questions, after reading this book. I will list out an email address here that you can use to communicate:

followhimwithus@gmail.com
If you'll be patient with me, I promise to answer every email!
- Jason

1
Let's start at the beginning

In the beginning….
Let's start at the beginning. The beginning of what? Should we start at the beginning of the Sermon on the Mount in Matthew 5? Should we start at the beginning of the book of Matthew? Should we start at the beginning of creation as we know it? The answer is YES – to all 3 questions!

If we start back in Genesis 1, we have the familiar words, "In the beginning, God created the heavens and the earth." We know and accept that God our Father existed before this moment….Jesus existed before this moment….the Spirit of God existed before this moment; but, this is what we, as humans, understand as the beginning of our creation. It's the beginning of time as we know it, or as we can understand it. We understand that this is the moment that our Earth was created, and we understand this story in Genesis 1 is when God created mankind.

Now, let's fast forward to the Gospel of John, chapter 1, verses 1-5 (NLT):

> In the beginning the Word already existed. The Word was with God, and the Word was God. ² He existed in the beginning with God. ³ God created everything through him, and nothing was created except through him. ⁴ The Word gave life to everything that was created, and his life brought light to everyone. ⁵ The light shines in the darkness, and the darkness can never extinguish it.

So, we learn here that Jesus already existed before Genesis 1. Jesus was with the Father in Heaven, and He is equal to God. We also learn that EVERYTHING was created through Jesus, and that He gave life to everything that was created. It is very important that we understand that Jesus has always been in existence with our Father God. He was not just a baby that was created when Mary became pregnant from the Holy Spirit. He wasn't created after the beginning of time to merely be a human that became our Savior. He is God. He is our Creator.

Why is this important? He is the ONLY human that has ever walked on this Earth that fully understands the will of God, the nature of God, as well as the instructions or commands of God. He is the only human that truly knows the Father, and He came to bridge the gap that sin created between us and the Father. In verse 1, it says the Word was God. This is huge for us! This means that we have a living, breathing human being that can tell us exactly what God wants and expects from us, and He can show us who the Father is!

In John 14, Jesus is trying to comfort His disciples after telling them that He will be "going away" to prepare eternity for them. When Thomas questions Jesus about this in John 14 verse 5, Jesus responds in verses 6-11 (NLT):

> ⁶ Jesus told him, "I am the way, the truth, and the life. No one can come to the Father except through me. ⁷ If you had really known me, you would know who my Father is. From now on, you do know him and have seen him!"
>
> ⁸ Philip said, "LORD, show us the Father, and we will be satisfied."
>
> ⁹ Jesus replied, "Have I been with you all this time, Philip, and yet you still don't know who I am? Anyone who has seen me has

seen the Father! So why are you asking me to show him to you? ¹⁰ Don't you believe that I am in the Father and the Father is in me? The words I speak are not my own, but my Father who lives in me does his work through me. ¹¹ Just believe that I am in the Father and the Father is in me. Or at least believe because of the work you have seen me do."

Pay attention to some key words that Jesus says here. **"If you had really known me, you would know who my Father is. From now on, you do know Him and have seen Him!"** Jesus is explaining to them that they have seen the Father – they know the Father through knowing Him. Yes, Jesus came to save us, and to reunite us with the Father – BUT, He also came to SHOW us the Father! Jesus tells Thomas in verse 9 – **"Anyone who has seen me has seen the Father!"**

This is very important for us to understand as we unpack what it means to know Jesus, as well as what it means to be known by Jesus. These verses, along with many others, establish the credibility that Jesus has to show us what the Father, Creator God wants from us, and what He expects from us. It will help us understand what it means to be known by the Creator Himself!

To know someone....

If we dig into the word "known" in the scripture referenced above, it's the Greek word "ginosko", which means to learn to know, to come to know, or to understand at the most intimate level. It's not simply just being aware of something, but it's a continual process of learning and understanding. This is important for us to understand as we begin this process of making sure that we are known by Jesus.

You may meet a person one time, shake their hand, exchange names, and start telling everyone that you "know" them. The reality is that you have made a new acquaintance, but simply meeting them doesn't mean that you really "know" them. How do you truly get to know them? We get to know them by starting to learn about that person, by spending time with that person, and by continuing to learn about that person over time. You start with the acquaintance – the meeting – but getting to know them, takes time and energy.

However, just because you take an interest in someone to learn more about them, doesn't necessarily mean that they know you. I want you to think of someone who is famous, maybe a sports star, a movie star, or a musician that is famous. You can watch that person perform in their field of expertise. You may hear them talk in a TV interview. You may read an autobiography or biography about them. You may follow them on social media and get to hear their voice daily. You are taking the time and energy to learn a lot about them. However, the reality is that you have some knowledge about who that person is, but you don't really "know" them. And most likely, they don't know anything about you. You may feel like you know them, but if you met them face to face, they know nothing about you. It has been completely one-sided.

As believers in Jesus, we have to make sure that we are not setting up the same or similar scenario. We can listen to sermons and podcasts about Jesus. We can listen to someone's testimony about Jesus. We can read the bible and all the red letters of where Jesus spoke. We can learn the traditional denominational aspects about Jesus, but at the end of the day, is it just knowledge? Is it just a one-way, one-sided relationship? I'm not saying that any of those things are wrong or bad. Each of those things can be very important in getting to know who Jesus is, but our goal is to be known by Him, not simply just to have "head knowledge" of who He is.

My hope is that as you read this, there will be a healthy tension that begins to develop around this question of whether or not Jesus will know you when you meet Him one day. I hope a tension builds that causes you to dig into scripture more and more to better understand and know who He is. I hope a new hunger develops to know Him more than you previously have known Him. I hope that you will take this serious as you explore if He will know you.

I also hope this tension doesn't turn into a negative tension, one of worry, fear, or rejection (not feeling good enough). My concern is that we don't talk about this enough as Christ followers, but this discussion is intended to create excitement to know more, not fear that you'll never get there. There is a beauty that when Jesus says these words, He's at the tail end of a famous sermon, called the Sermon on the Mount.

Why is that sermon important??
In Matthew 7:21-23, Jesus says:

[21] "Not everyone who calls out to me, 'LORD! LORD!' will enter the Kingdom of Heaven. Only those who actually do the will of my Father in heaven will enter. [22] On judgment day many will say to me, 'LORD! LORD! We prophesied in your name and cast out demons in your name and performed many miracles in your name.' [23] But I will reply, 'I never knew you. Get away from me, you who break God's laws.'

Did you see what He just said? These people Prophesied in His name – they cast out demons in His name – they performed Miracles in His name, but He still said "I never knew you…..get away from Me…." How can someone do such incredible things in the name of Jesus, but still fall under the category of not being known by Jesus?

I have good news! When Jesus says this in Chapter 7, He is near the end of this famous sermon. He has just laid out a great Blueprint of what He expects from us as His followers, and we'll spend the majority of this book covering what He laid out in this sermon, covered in Matthew, from chapter 5 to chapter 7. Before He gives the warning, He has given us incredible insight into what He expects of us. A Good Father, like our Creator God, will never give a warning until He has made it clear what He expects us to do.

Even the demons believe and know Jesus….
Maybe you have read until this point, and you think I'm being a little too dramatic about the desire for Jesus to know each of us, as believers. I'll go ahead and drop a little bombshell on you if you think that your belief in Jesus is all you need. Even the demons believe in Jesus…Even the demons know Jesus. I'm going to give you 4 examples with scripture to prove this point:

1. In Acts 19, we have a story where Jews are traveling from town to town, casting out evil spirits (demons) in Jesus name. In Acts 19, verse 15, it says [15] But one time when they tried it, the evil spirit replied, "I know Jesus, and I know Paul, but who are you?"
2. In Mark 1, we have a story of where Jesus is teaching in the synagogue on the Sabbath. In Mark 1, verses 23-24, it says [23] Suddenly, a man in the synagogue who was possessed by an evil spirit cried out, [24] "Why are you interfering with us, Jesus of Nazareth? Have you come to destroy us? I know who you are—the Holy One of God!"
3. In Matthew 8, verses 28-33, we have the story of the two demon possessed men who were so violent that no one could travel through the area where they inhabited. In verse 29, when they saw Jesus, it says [29] They began screaming at him, "Why are you interfering with us, Son of God? Have you come here to torture us before God's appointed time?" Not only did they know who Jesus was, they knew a lot about Him! They knew He was the Son of God. They knew He had power over them. They knew that He had an appointed time, and they knew that His appointed time had not come yet. They didn't just know Jesus – they knew scripture and prophecies about Jesus.
4. In James 2:19, James, the brother of Jesus, who is also the leader of the early Jesus following church in Jerusalem says "[19] You say you have faith, for you believe that there is one God. Good for you! Even the demons believe this, and they tremble in terror."

Is it enough to know???

We go back to the first question. Is it enough to know Jesus? Is it enough to believe in Jesus? Well, we just covered 3 examples of when demons knew Jesus and believed in Jesus, but their fate was definitely not eternity with Him in paradise. Then, we have James saying "Good for you. Even the demons believe…..oh, and they tremble".

So, what is the difference between the demons belief in Jesus, and our belief in Jesus? The demons feared Him; or I should say – the demons fear Him. But, the demons were not and are not obedient to Jesus. Knowing Jesus is important, but we are about to embark on a journey of the importance of our **OBEDIENCE** to the Son of God, which in turn, equates to our obedience to the Creator God.

The demons tremble in fear. My hope is that we will take the time to get to know Jesus to the level that we have so much awe and respect for Him that we will search out the areas of our lives where we are disobedient to Him. Not only will we search out those areas, but we will make the changes necessary to correct those areas of our lives. On that day of judgment, I don't want to tremble in fear like the demons do. I want to tremble in the awe and respect of the Savior of the world! I want to stand in awe of The Man, who gave His life, allowing His body to be broken and allowing His blood to be spilled out, for YOU and for me.

He has such an incredible love for you and for me that He laid His life down for us. In return, let's take the time to understand what He wants in return for that sacrifice. In my faith-based salvation, there is nothing that I can do to earn the free gift of salvation that He gave to me. But, because of His love and sacrifice, I want to do everything I can to know Him more and more. I don't want to just know about Him, but I want to know Him intimately, and I want to serve Him, and obey Him, and live a life of faith worthy of the sacrifice He made for me. How about you? We have to start here at this point of dedication, faith, and love for Him – if we want to fully understand how to be known by Him!

Questions and Application for Chapter 1
1. Do you believe that Jesus is equal to the Father, the Creator?
2. Do you believe that Jesus is the only human that has ever truly understood and known the Father?
3. Can you think of any areas of your life where you know you need to be more obedient to Jesus?
4. Are you willing to make changes when God shows you something that needs to be changed?
5. Challenge – As you read this book, and as we dig into scripture, please write down and take notes on the areas of your life that you need to evaluate and change.

Prayer
"Our Father, who is in heaven, thank you for giving us your Word. Thank you for giving us your Son, so that we could know You! Thank you for giving us your written words of instruction, so that we can know what you expect from us. Father, I pray that as we read through this Sermon on the Mount, You will show us the areas that we need to change. Give us the courage to make the changes. Give us the courage to go against the world or to go against what we've been taught, if that's what it takes to be more obedient to You. Help us to learn more and more about you, through Your Son Jesus's sermon. Help us to grasp what You need each of us to know so that we can be truly known by You!"

2

Matthew, the disciple

Why Matthew?
Why do you think that Jesus chose Matthew to write a detailed account of His sermon? Let's look at what we know about Matthew, the disciple. First, we know that Matthew was a Jewish man, who served the Roman government as a tax collector. Matthew 9:9 says:

⁹ As Jesus was walking along, he saw a man named Matthew sitting at his tax collector's booth. "Follow me and be my disciple," Jesus said to him. So Matthew got up and followed him.

We have the same story in Mark 2:14 and in Luke 5:27. We will see the name Levi, but that is the same person we call Matthew.

Mark 2:14 says:

¹⁴ As he walked along, he saw Levi son of Alphaeus sitting at his tax collector's booth. "Follow me and be my disciple," Jesus said to him. So Levi got up and followed him.

Luke 5:27 says:

²⁷ Later, as Jesus left the town, he saw a tax collector named Levi sitting at his tax collector's booth. "Follow me and be my disciple," Jesus said to him.

All 3 introductions of Matthew describe Jesus finding Matthew at his tax collector booth. This means that Matthew would have been hated by most of the Jewish people. Tax collectors were despised by the Jews. So, we have a Jewish man, helping the Romans take tax money from the Jewish people. WOW! For the Jewish people, the amount of betrayal and selfishness would be a nearly unforgivable thing!

But, what else do we know about a tax collector? A tax collector would take PERFECT NOTES. A tax collector would keep impeccable records. Their details would be exact. Have you ever stopped and thought about this? Jesus chose a man to be one of His disciples who would have been despised, but he would have been a man who would take time to make sure his notes and facts about Jesus were perfect as he wrote down the records. I believe it's important to take this into account as we look at the Sermon on the Mount, written by a man named Matthew, chosen by Jesus because he would write the story correctly. He would write the Sermon on the Mount onto paper, just as Jesus had told it.

If Jesus is going to choose a book of the bible to tell us what we need to do so that He will know us, it makes sense that He would choose the man that would get the story down correctly, so that we aren't left to wonder what Jesus meant by those crucial words. I'm not sure about you, but that is very comforting to me! Jesus loves you and me so much that He died for us. Our Creator God loves us so much that He sent His only Son to die for us. Jesus expects us to do something with our belief in Him, and He lays it out for us through the writings of a man that would write it EXACTLY how Jesus said it! That's incredible!! There's no room for confusion. We aren't left to wonder if we got the whole story. We can rest, knowing that Jesus chose the perfect person to write down the story – the story that includes the instructions we would need to be known by Jesus!!

Not only do I find comfort here, but I find comfort in knowing that Jesus chose Matthew, not based on Matthew's past, but rather on who Matthew could and would be! For me, this book is about your life from this day forward. The past, no matter how bad it was, will only be a part of the testimony from this day forward! I hope you find as much excitement and motivation in these two things as I do!

The Will of the Father...

Just before Jesus says those words in verses 22 and 23 that create the question of "will Jesus know me?", Matthew records a crucial statement from Jesus in verse 21 - [21]"Not everyone who calls out to me, 'Lord! Lord!' will enter the Kingdom of Heaven. Only those who actually do the will of my Father in heaven will enter."

Jesus gives us a hint in that statement of what it takes to be known by Him, and it's a huge hint. Only those who do the will of my Father will enter the Kingdom of Heaven. So, what exactly is the will of the Father? Jesus loves you and me so much that He chose a man like Matthew, who would take exact notes, to spend 3 chapters laying out the will of the Father to us! I'm trying to make this point because it gives me such great comfort to know that the answer to the greatest question we could ever ask, has been laid out and entrusted to a man who would write it exactly the way Jesus said it. I hope it gives you the same comfort.

The Lineage of Jesus....

As Matthew begins his account of the story of Jesus, He starts out in Chapter 1, verses 1-17, laying out the lineage of Jesus. Why would the meticulous note taker start here? Matthew starts with the lineage of Jesus because it is important for the reader to be assured that Jesus was a descendant of King David, which was a prophesied requirement of the Messiah (Savior). Before recording what Jesus says, Matthew needs to set the stage that the lineage of Jesus proves that He's a descendant of both Abraham and David, two crucial pieces of the ancestry puzzle that Jesus needed to have. Matthew would have been writing to a crowd of people that knew the prophecies of the expected Messiah, so he starts there to set up the story for Jesus.

Then, Matthew explains the birth of Jesus, starting with how a virgin, named Mary, became pregnant by the power of the Holy Spirit. He then explains how Joseph, Mary's fiancé, was planning to privately break off his engagement to Mary, due to her pregnancy, until an angel appeared to Joseph to explain to him that Mary was pregnant with Jesus, who had come to be the Savior of the world. At this point, Joseph knew that this fulfilled a direct prophecy about the Messiah, given by the great prophet, Isaiah.

Next, in Chapter 2, Matthew covers the birth of Jesus, and why they had to flee to Egypt. These are important details for the early readers of Matthew, who understood all the prophecies about the Messiah. Matthew had to take the time to set up who Jesus is, before just jumping into Jesus's famous sermon.

Chapter 3 focuses on John the Baptist, how he taught on repentance, and how he was also a fulfillment of the second coming of Elijah. John was sent to prepare the way for Jesus, and we see the story of how he baptized Jesus.

Then, in Chapter 4, before Jesus picks His disciples, before He starts His ministry, Jesus is tempted in the wilderness by satan. After 40 days of fasting, when Jesus is at a very weak human moment, the enemy comes in and tempts Jesus with worldly things, trying to get Jesus to give up His purpose.

After temptation, Jesus picks His disciples, begins His ministry, and crowds begin to follow Him as He traveled the countryside, teaching and healing.

Matthew spends time setting up who Jesus is before jumping into the Sermon on the Mount in Chapter 5. My goal was to cover Chapters 1-4 quickly. They are very important for setting up the story, but we want to get to the meat of the sermon, right? Before we move on, I want to go back to Chapter 1 and make sure that we don't miss a few very important verses. These are verses that we often read quickly, without understanding the depth of one word that is used.

True Intimacy...
Back in Matthew 1, verses 24-25, it says

²⁴ When Joseph woke up, he did as the angel of the LORD commanded and took Mary as his wife. ²⁵ But he did not have sexual relations with her until her son was born. And Joseph named him Jesus.

Now, please be patient with me while I explain this next piece. Please promise that you will read this completely before thinking I'm going down a crazy tangent. In verse 25, in the New Living Translation (NLT), it says that he (Joseph) did not have "sexual relations" with Mary until Jesus was born. The Greek word used in Matthew 1:25 for sexual relations is "ginosko", the same exact word that we discussed in Chapter 1 of this book. It's the same Greek word that we often translate to "know". To remind you, that word means to learn to know, to come to know, or to understand at the most intimate level. Often, a Greek word (most of the New Testament) or a Hebrew word (most of the Old Testament) means much more than the equivalent English word that we translate it to. In this case, we have the same word "ginosko" that Jesus uses when He says in Matthew 7 verse 23 "But I will reply, I never KNEW you".

Why am I pointing this out? God never intended for sex to be looked at the way that our world sees it now. God's original design for sexual intercourse was to produce offspring to populate the Earth, and it was meant for two people AND ONLY those two people to KNOW each other at a level that no one else would know. It was designed to create a "oneness" and a unity between two humans that should only exist between those two humans. Part of the intent and use of the word ginosko in this scripture is to show that sexual intercourse was intended to create a bond where a man would know his wife better and more completely than he would know any other human. And the same for his wife – that she would know her husband better and more completely than she would know any other human. I know that talking about sex "in church" is weird and taboo, but God didn't create that weirdness. It is our enemy, the adversary, satan, that twisted and perverted the original design into what our world sees it as today. God intended this level of knowing to be a wonderful and beautiful level of understanding, bonding, and unity that would be special and sacred between a man and a woman in marriage. The enemy, satan, has twisted God's design to be the selfish, self-seeking gratification that we often think of in today's world.

Understanding the true meaning of this word 'ginosko' here in Matthew 1:25 helps us understand that Jesus has a desire for us to "know" Him and for Him to "know" us at an intimate level that no one else could. We have to understand the true meaning of the words, as we get the weird, worldly context out of our heads. Jesus desires to know everything about you. He wants to know you more intimately than anyone else in this world knows you.

It's not simply that Jesus wants you to know everything about Him, but He wants you to know how He thinks, how He feels, how He processes things – He wants you to get to know Him at a level where you know more about Him than anyone else on this planet. And equally, that's the level that He wants to know you! Isn't that exciting? The Messiah, the Savior of the world, Immanuel (God is with us) wants to know YOU, like no one else on this planet knows you. That should be exciting for each of us!

Unfortunately, that can be a bit scary for each of us, if we are hiding some dark secrets, thoughts, or actions within our hearts. You might be thinking – "well, I have thoughts in my head that I don't want anyone to know……" or "I have thoughts in my head that I'm ashamed of…." That's the beauty of where we are going with this book. Jesus spends the entire Sermon on the Mount telling us what He expects of us, and much of the teaching compares or contrasts our outward actions with our inward thoughts. You might say our outward actions versus our 'hearts'. Jesus doesn't expect you to be perfect, but He does expect us to do some things.

Part of being obedient to Him is allowing Him to change the way we think, which will ultimately change the way we act.

I want to encourage you to be patient with yourself. Don't look at the things Jesus lays out, get overwhelmed, and give up. Try and pick one thing to work on at a time. As you tackle each area of your "heart", and as you allow Jesus to make changes in that area, you are allowing Him to know you more and more. As He shapes you, you are allowing Him to know you.

This is personal for me...

One last thing on intimacy before we move on. As humans, we have different levels of intimacy. After reading this book, you will know me better. You will hopefully know and see the passion I have to follow Jesus with everything in my being. But, my friends know me a little better than the average reader will. My church family knows me a little better than my other friends. My children know me better than my church family knows me. My wife knows me better than my children know me. As the circle, so to speak, gets closer, the "knowing" gets deeper. But, only Jesus knows me completely. He's the only one that knows every thought, every intention, every problem, every praise, etc. That sounds great, right?

Well.....in 2012 (and before), I wasn't chasing after Jesus the way I am today. In fact, I tried to shut Him out as much as possible from knowing me, because I didn't want Him to know the real me. I could put on a great Christian mask, say the right things, quote the right scriptures, and act the part. But, the reality is that I had a lot of hidden thoughts and desires that didn't line up with His teachings. I knew that. Jesus knew that. However, many around me, even close people, didn't know the extent of the evil within me. But....... one day, I made a decision to allow Him in to those evil areas. I allowed Jesus to see the ugly parts of me, and I embarked on what has now been an 11-year journey (at the time of this writing). I decided that I wanted to know who Jesus truly is. I had head knowledge of Him, pretty much from birth. I've never not known who Jesus is. But, I didn't know Him at an intimate level. I knew of him, but I didn't KNOW Him intimately.

I have worked literally every day since that year to allow Jesus to know me, to search me, and to change me. Some areas were easy, but many were hard and took time. I believe that I will spend the rest of my life on Earth, trying every day to get to know Him a little better. And, my hope and prayer, is that I will spend every day, allowing Him to know me better. My point is that intimacy is a thing that is built with intention, and it takes time.

If you are married, I want you to think about your spouse. You knew that person before you were married. Each year that you are married, you know them more and more, right? Over time, each of you has changed, maybe for the better....maybe for the worse. Here's the beauty of our relationship with Jesus. He was defined before time as we know it, and scripture tells us that He doesn't change – He's the same yesterday, today, and tomorrow! And – He's perfect! His desire is to know you. His desire is to help you make the changes in your heart and in your actions that you need to make, as you and Jesus grow closer together. His goal is to have an intimacy with you that will be greater than any other relationship you have!

I was Matthew, so to speak. I chased the dollar more than I chased Jesus. I did evil things. I thought evil things. I was not worthy of being known by Jesus. But, one day, He saw me at my "booth", and He said, "Jason, Follow Me." Like Matthew, I dropped it all, and changed my life for Him. I'm still not perfect, but I can give you the hope that you can be different – that you can be changed – that your evil can become Holy – and that you can be and will be known by Jesus! This is the blueprint that I have used, and I'll do my best to write the story EXACTLY like Matthew did!

Questions and Application for Chapter 2
1. Are you excited to start this journey, or are you terrified of the thought of Jesus knowing you intimately?
2. Do you have thoughts that you don't want Jesus to know?
3. Do you feel like you are good enough for Jesus to know you?
4. Do you feel like there is anything in your past that would disqualify you from being known?
5. Challenge – Don't hide your "ugly" stuff from Jesus. He already knows! Make a decision today to be different. Make a decision today to leave your "tax booth" and follow Him with everything you have!

Prayer
"Father, thank you for showing us how to go from a despised tax collector to a disciple of Jesus! Thank you for giving us the example of Matthew and the other broken men that made the same decision to follow Jesus. Thank you for being a merciful Father, who allows us to change! I bind up any fear in Jesus's name that would keep me from giving all my thoughts and actions to Jesus. I bind up any rejection in Jesus's name that would make me feel like I'm not good enough to change for you, Father. You sent your Son to die for me. Thank you for loving me so much to do that!"

3

The Sermon on the Mount

The heart behind the actions...

At the end of Matthew 4, we are told that Jesus began traveling across the region, teaching and healing. Verse 23 says "And He healed every kind of disease and illness". What do you think happens when you come out of nowhere and start miraculously healing everyone and claiming to be the long-awaited Messiah? It draws a crowd! That's what we see happening at the beginning of Matthew chapter 5.

The prophets of God have been silent for 400 years. Then, John the Baptist shows up and draws a crowd with his message and with his baptisms. Next, Jesus comes on the scene and starts teaching and healing EVERY kind of disease and sickness. That will draw a crowd!

As the crowd is drawn, and Jesus begins to teach, we will see a theme that I mentioned in Chapter 2. We quickly see that the things that He cares about revolve around inward things, like our hearts or our thoughts. You will notice that the people 'who are left out' from being known had great actions, but those actions were all about drawing attention to self…"Look what I did!"

Jesus is saying, Yes, you did good things. But, you did these things to bring attention to yourself. Your heart was not in the right place. It's not about what the world sees you do. It's not about what your friends or family see you do. We can do a lot of the "right" things with the "wrong" heart. Much of this discussion will be about our hearts, and us allowing Jesus to make changes to our hearts. More simply stated – it will be about allowing Jesus to change the way we think. Our thoughts produce actions, but now we do these actions with the right heart.

This is not really a new concept, in terms of what we expect from our Creator. Back in 1 Samuel 16, Samuel has been given a task to find the person that will replace Saul as King of God's people. In verse 7, it says:

> [7] But the LORD said to Samuel, "Don't judge by his appearance or height, for I have rejected him. The LORD doesn't see things the way you see them. People judge by outward appearance, but the LORD looks at the heart."

This was written roughly 1,000 years before Jesus spoke in Matthew 5. So, whether we look back 3,000 years to the writings of Samuel, or we look back 2,000 years to the writings of Matthew, or we look at our world today in the 21st century, there are a few things that have not changed. First of all, the world, or people in the world, judge by outward appearance. It was happening then, and it still happens today. People of the world judge by what they see. At the same time, another more important truth has not changed. Whether we are talking about God, the Creator, or Jesus, the Messiah, we see that a different thing is used to judge a person. God told Samuel, "I look at the heart of the person". Jesus tells us here in Matthew that He is focused on our hearts.

It is important, too, for us to see here in Matthew that we can do good things in His name – the name of Jesus – but have the wrong heart and intentions behind it. Jesus doesn't care what you look like....how tall you are....what you weigh....how good you look at church....how many scriptures you can quote......Jesus cares about how much you allow Him to change your heart. He cares about how much you let Him change and mold your heart to fit into the Will of the Father. This will produce good things, done in His Name, for the right reasons and for the right purpose.

The Blessings....

The world gives us a standard of success, but Jesus often directly contrasts the world's standard of success to explain the Kingdom of God's standard for success. As He begins the Sermon on the Mount, we find what I'm going to call "the blessings". If your bible has titles above sections, just before verse 3 of Matthew 5, you might see the words "The Beatitudes". You may have seen or heard that word before, but not understood what it means. It means Supreme Blessedness. In other words, it's a fancy, Christian word for "The Blessings".

Now, before we dig into what the Blessings are, let's make sure that we understand what the word "blessing" means.

I'm not sure where you live, but I'm "blessed" to live in the state of Tennessee, in the Southeastern United States. In the south, we have this word, Blessed. I just used it to describe my situation – I'm blessed, in my opinion, to live in an incredible state. I used that term to mean that I feel fortunate to live here. It's a term we use often, but it is not what the word blessing means.

Also, we have a phrase that we use in the south, and we use it often – "Bless your heart". When we think that someone has suffered through a circumstance that was unfair, or they have endured something tough or tragic, we will say "bless your heart". It's a term we use when we feel bad for someone or their situation. Also, if we were to be completely honest, it's a term that is sometimes used when we think someone is foolish or dumb....well, bless your heart. But, once again, in all these cases, this is not what the word blessing really means.

Oh, and I can't forget that we all make sure we say a "blessing" before we eat each meal. Thanking God for our food is important, but it's once again the wrong use of the word.

So, we have this word "blessed" or "bless", and we often use it to mean I'm fortunate....I'm happy....I'm lucky....or we use it to mean "I feel sorry for you"....or worse. Or, we use it to describe thankfulness for our food. These uses of the word blessed have become figures of speech, and we've lost the true meaning of the word.

Another use I'll describe before moving on to the true meaning....is when we use the word "blessed" to sound like a good Christian. "How are you today, Jason?" "I'm blessed!" Or maybe we'll tell someone to have a "Blessed day". Neither of those uses are wrong, but I've noticed in the South, we've begun to use those terms to covertly insinuate that we are Christians. Someone will tell me that they are "Blessed and Highly Favored". Or, they will say "Be Blessed", and immediately, I think – "Hey, this person must be a Christ follower because they said Blessed!"

I'm trying to make a point that we have a word that we use often, but I don't think we know the true meaning. So, let's look at the true meaning of the word Blessed, as Jesus uses it here in Matthew 5. In verses 3-12, Jesus uses this word 9 times. It's the English word "blessed", but it is the Greek word "makarios". As you might have guessed, the word makarios has a deeper meaning than just being fortunate or happy or one of the other things listed above.

First, it can mean Holy, which really means to be "set apart". If you are holy, it means that you are set apart from something else. Our Creator, Our Father, is Holy. He is set apart as the ONE and ONLY God. He expects us to be Holy, which means we are set apart from the world. We are different, or at least we are expected to be different than those around us who don't know and who don't follow Jesus.

If we go a little deeper into the meaning of "makarios" or "blessed", it means to be made larger, or to enlarge. Another way of saying this or thinking about this is that the word blessed means that God is making Himself larger to us, or you could say that when we are blessed, we are getting more of God.

It is very important that we understand the deeper meaning of the word "blessed" as we begin to read what Jesus is trying to tell us here in Matthew 5, verses 3-12.

Jesus starts this famous sermon by telling us some situations where we are blessed. He's describing the things that will set us apart from the world. He's describing the things that enlarge our benefits from the Father. He's describing the things that get us more of God!

Matthew 5:3-12 (NLT)

3 "God blesses those who are poor and realize their need for him,
for the Kingdom of Heaven is theirs.
4 God blesses those who mourn,
for they will be comforted.
5 God blesses those who are humble,
for they will inherit the whole earth.
6 God blesses those who hunger and thirst for justice,
for they will be satisfied.
7 God blesses those who are merciful,
for they will be shown mercy.
8 God blesses those whose hearts are pure,
for they will see God.
9 God blesses those who work for peace,
for they will be called the children of God.
10 God blesses those who are persecuted for doing right,
for the Kingdom of Heaven is theirs.
11 "God blesses you when people mock you and persecute you and lie about you and say all sorts of evil things against you because you are my followers. 12 Be happy about it! Be very glad! For a great reward awaits you in heaven. And remember, the ancient prophets were persecuted in the same way."

The world versus The Kingdom...

We will spend an entire chapter, breaking down each of the verses that you just read, but there is a theme that develops here that will be carried through the rest of Jesus's sermon. We basically have a view of life from one of two viewpoints. One option is that our thoughts of happiness or of success will be viewed from a worldly perspective. In that perspective, we will compare our situation to those around us. We will make a judgment on how good or bad our life is, based on our condition compared to others around us or others that we know. The second option is that our thoughts of happiness or of success will be viewed from a Kingdom of God perspective. This perspective will contrast completely with a world view, most of the time. From this point forward, I'll refer to this as a "world" view versus a "kingdom" view. Please know that when I use the word kingdom, I'm referring to the Kingdom of God.

Every circumstance of our daily life can be viewed through the lens of the world or through the lens of the kingdom. For example, in the world, success is often based on position, power, and money. In contrast, kingdom success is exactly the opposite. I want to give some biblical examples of how the kingdom view is the opposite.

As John the Baptist was becoming more popular, crowds of people were swarming to hear his message. He had disciples that were following him. He is gaining power. He is gaining popularity. But, he always had a kingdom mindset. He understood that his role was to prepare the way for Jesus. He told the religious leaders in John 1 verse 23, "I am a voice shouting in the wilderness, 'Clear the way for the LORD's coming!'" Then, in John 1 verse 27, he says "Though his ministry follows mine, I'm not even worthy to be his slave and untie the straps of his sandal". John had a Kingdom view of his own life. Although he was gaining in worldly popularity, he remained humble, understanding that his role was not worldly, but secondary to the role of Jesus. In John 3, verse 30, John says something that I think shows just how 'anti-worldly' he was. He says "He (Jesus) must become greater and greater and I must become less and less." In the world's view, becoming greater and greater is the goal. For John to say Jesus will become greater….and he (John) would become less – that goes against everything the world calls success. He was failing by the world's standard, by giving up his fame for someone better. But, let's look at John from a kingdom perspective. John was willing to understand that he was the person to introduce Jesus to the world. John understood that he wasn't worthy to be Jesus's slave. John was willing to lower himself so that Jesus could be made greater. John was willing to give up his own disciples (followers) and allow them to follow Jesus. John was willing to give up his life to speak the truth about God's kingdom.

By the world's standard, John failed. John gave up what he was building. BUT – by the kingdom standard, John is a great prophet, earning incredible eternal rewards. The world would call him a failure. 2,000 years later, we revere John, from a kingdom perspective!

John is an example of giving up power and popularity, but what about money. I stated earlier that the world views money as a success criteria. Not trying to get too far ahead, but in Matthew 6, Jesus shows us a different kingdom measure. We will wait and dig into this in a later chapter, but Jesus says don't store your treasure on Earth…store it up in Heaven. We'll cover more of what that means as we cover that chapter, but I wanted to use it as an example to contrast that worldly wealth is different than kingdom wealth. Worldly wealth is about how much money you can make. Kingdom wealth has NOTHING to do with money – unless you are using your money to help others or to help the needy.

A final example I'll give has to do with what the Jewish people in Jesus's time viewed or perceived the Messiah would be versus what He actually was. They had a worldly view of a Messiah that would come as a powerful military king. This king was expected to come and to relieve the oppression of the Roman tyrants, who had conquered their land. But, as we know, Jesus shows up pretty much as the exact opposite. Jesus is humble and meek (not weak!). Jesus gives up His life for each of us. The King of the Kingdom that they received was a lot different than the warrior king that they were expecting.

I hope you see my point. Worldly success is much different than Kingdom success. That is going to be the theme of Jesus's sermon, as He lays out what is success in the Kingdom of God. This is laying the foundation of what it means to be known by Jesus. God is a Holy God, set apart from all other things in the world. God calls us as Christ followers to be holy as well – set apart – different from the world. Jesus is about to tell us how we are set apart, and how we get more of God!!!

Questions and Application for Chapter 3
1. Do you judge people by how they look, before getting to know their heart?
2. Have you ever been frustrated that people only judge you by your appearance or social status, instead of looking at your heart?
3. Have you been tempted to compromise your Kingdom success in order to achieve worldly success?
4. Is it hard for you to give up worldly success to achieve Kingdom success?
5. Challenge – Make sure that you look past someone's appearance to see the quality of their heart. They may look great on the outside, but they may have a dark and dirty heart. Or, they may look lowly and unimportant on the outside, while having a beautiful and special heart for God!

Prayer
"Father, help me to look at the heart of people instead of looking at what the world would call successful, or pretty, or wealthy. Help me to see the heart of the people I'm with so that I will know if they are kingdom focused or worldly focused. Father, please help mold my heart to be a heart that You would want, no matter what the world thinks of me. Please help me to evaluate my worldly desires so that I can change them and give them up to be more Kingdom focused!"

4

Understanding the "Blessings"

The poor…the poor in spirit…(Matthew 5:3)
Jesus starts off in verse 3, with "God blesses those who are poor and realize their need for him, for the Kingdom of Heaven is theirs."

I'm using the New Living Translation. I will often reference many different translations, but it's key to go back to the original Greek or Hebrew text to get deeper meaning when we are trying to fully understand a scripture. For everyday reading, I use the NLT because it is easier to read. My NLT bible says "God blesses those who are poor". But, if you are using a different translation, like the NIV or the King James, you will see a different phrase – "God blesses those who are poor in spirit". So, which is correct? Does He bless those who are poor? Or does He bless those who are poor in spirit? The answer is "both".

If you dig into the Greek word here (ptochos), it means someone who is reduced to begging. It means someone who is destitute of wealth, influence, position, or honor. It means the lowly, the afflicted, the helpless, the powerless. When you add in the word spirit here (pneuma), to make the phrase poor in spirit, it means that you don't have the worldly means to be educated.

These are the first words recorded in the first 'sermon' that Jesus preaches. The first words out of His mouth set up a stark contrast to what His world would have known as success. In that culture, remember that He was talking to Jewish people. Success would have been measured in money or in knowledge. How much do you have? How much do you know? What is your career? How much livestock do you own? How much formal training and knowledge do you have? These were all things that would have driven success back in Jesus's time, from a worldly perspective.

Now, Jesus shows up, and the first words out of His mouth set up one of the biggest contrasts of the culture of the time, and these words set up the theme of the sermon. Jesus is saying – if you want to be Holy – if you want to be Set Apart by God, you need to realize that the Kingdom of God has different standards than the world does. It never says that money is bad or that success is bad, but He is telling us what is important to our Father.

In Jesus's world, as well as in today's world, money was viewed as a measurement of success, and education was viewed as a measurement of success. People of that time (just like today) would not have thought they were important or successful if they were poor and uneducated. Certainly, they wouldn't see a beggar as successful! But those who are beggars in this world understand that they need something else. Jesus is saying that those who are less fortunate – those that realize how much they need God's help – those are the ones that get more of Him! Remember, to be blessed means to get more of God. He is enlarged to those that are blessed. To be blessed, means to be set apart. Jesus is telling us that the world will view money as a blessing, but those who are beggars (physically, mentally, emotionally, and/or spiritually), those people know how much they need God. People with money will often put their faith in the security that they perceive money offers them. But, those that don't have money to put their faith in for that false security, have to rely more on their faith in God, and thus, they get more of Him! They are the ones that are blessed! Worldly success does not give you the Kingdom of Heaven. Relying on your faith in Jesus...relying on your faith in the Father...that's what gets you the Kingdom of Heaven!

I want to give a personal story on this one. As I went through high school, college, and then into my career of sales in the tech industry, from 1990 till 2012, I lived out the model of worldly success:

1. Straight A student at a private Christian high school (1990-1994); graduated with honors
2. Full Scholarship to college and straight A's through college (1994-1998); graduated with honors
3. Quickly rose in the ranks of one of the world's largest tech companies, starting out with a salary of $45,000 in 1998, and ending with nearly $2 million in salary/commissions by the end of the year 2012.

From a worldly perspective, I was the model of success. I had the education, and the money! Here's the problem. If I look back over my life, I was the closest to God – to Jesus – in terms of faith – before high school. I was more faithful to God in high school than I was in college. I was more faithful in college than I was once I entered my career. The farther I climbed the ladder of worldly success, the farther I got away from the Kingdom of God and my faith. I never lost faith in Jesus. Honestly, I can never remember a time in my life that I didn't know Jesus. But, by 2012, I realized that I knew less and less about Him, and He would say that He didn't know me at all.

Maybe I should have mentioned all this in the Introduction or in Chapter 1, but this journey to understand how to be known by Jesus, stems from my personal journey. Most that know me now don't know the man I used to be. You wouldn't want to know that man! But, if you did know him, you'd see how much Jesus has changed me. I didn't mention this earlier because this book is NOT about me. It's about Jesus. It's about you and Jesus. It's about you being known by Jesus. I will continue to work every day to be known more and more by Him, but I want the same for you! I may not know you, but I love you, and I'm rooting for you to be known by Jesus!

When I had money – worldly success – I was rotting away internally. Now, I have pretty much given all my wealth away by doing ministry for 11 years, and my faith in God is stronger now than it ever has been. I realize that I need Him. That's what Jesus is getting at here. When we realize our need for God, for Jesus, instead of putting our faith in worldly things, that's when we get BLESSED! That's when we receive the Kingdom of God!!!

Some of you may read this and realize that you need to re-prioritize a few things in your life. You may be like I was, and realize that you are blessed by the world's standard, but not by the kingdom's standard. My hope is that this will begin a similar journey for you, as it did for me.

On the other hand, some of you may be having a "light bulb" moment, where God is showing you that you are in a better place than you thought! By the world's standard, you are nothing, or maybe you have nothing, or maybe you struggle from day to day to make ends meet. But, by the kingdom's standard, you are exactly where you want and need to be – BLESSED!

If you need to make changes, please have the courage and dedication to make those changes. If your eyes are opened to the fact that you are exactly where God wants you to be, YOU GET MORE OF GOD!!!!! YOU ARE TRULY BLESSED!

Those who mourn....God blesses those who mourn...(Matthew 5:4)

How many of you have lost a loved one due to death? Most, if not all of us, have. Maybe a dear friend has passed away. Maybe a spouse has passed away. Maybe you lost a pet that was special to you. The emotions that come with mourning and sadness, while a very natural response, are often difficult to control and get through.

It doesn't have to be a death. It could be a lost relationship (friend, spouse, mentor). Mourning is a natural thing that happens anytime that we lose something that is special to us. Mourning is a process of learning how to live a new life without that person or without that thing in our life. Each situation is different. Each person is different. The length and depth of mourning is different, but all people will experience this emotion and will have to go through this process at different times during their lives.

Let's be honest here – as humans, we don't like to see people mourn. If we see someone crying or we see someone sad, we tend to want to do one of two things. We either stay away from them because we don't know what to say, OR, we go overboard, trying to comfort and cheer up that person. We may think, "What can I do or say to cheer that person up?". We may tell them to stop crying. We may point out some positive things that we know about them. We may try to bring up something funny. We do these things with love, with mercy, and with compassion, because we don't like to see people hurting, emotionally. We don't like to see people sad.

BUT, Jesus tells us here in Matthew 5 that God blesses those who mourn. Let's remember our deeper definition of the word "bless". God gives more of Himself to those that are mourning. God enlarges Himself to those that are mourning. God sets you apart (holy) if you are mourning.

This may (and should) change how we view mourning. It's out of a good heart that we don't want to see people sad, or mourning, but if we don't allow them that opportunity, we are robbing them of a blessing. We should embrace their mourning! My hope is that you will think about this the next time you are mourning, or the next time that you see someone mourning. Encourage yourself or that person with the simple realization that God is blessing them in that moment!

Those who are humble....God blesses those who are humble...(Matthew 5:5)

Can we be honest with each other here? Being humble can be one of the hardest things we experience as humans. The temptation to be proud – to carry pride – seems to be a born in, sinful condition, that even the best of Christ followers will struggle with for an entire lifetime.

We are born with pride, and it's a daily battle for each of us. In fact, I will go so far as to say that we live in a world where pride is at an all-time high. That puts humility at possibly an all-time low. If we aren't following Jesus, which I would call being completely worldly, then the world is going to always be teaching us to do what we want, do what pleases us, and then take all the credit when things go in a successful direction. The two things that I just described about the world would be called selfishness and pride.

However, all throughout scripture, we are given a different model. We are given a model of laying down our selfishness, serving others, and then giving all credit to the Father in Heaven! Jesus tells us that everything that we do in His name is to bring Glory to the Father. As a follower of Jesus, we need to strive to constantly expose pride in our lives and continually make changes to turn our pride into humility. Again, there is no doubt that this one is hard. There is no doubt that this one definitely goes against the "world". There is no doubt that most of us will be in this battle until we die or until Jesus comes back to get us.

Here, Jesus gives us a little double incentive to work on our pride. He says, not only will you get more of God when you are humble, not only will He enlarge Himself to you when you are humble, you will inherit the earth. That's a pretty big promise! Every day, the worldly are trying to expand their earthly kingdom, so to speak. Jesus will come back and reign this Earth for 1,000 years before the New Heaven and the New Earth are created for our eternity with Jesus. I believe that Jesus is telling us that humbleness not only gets you more of God today, but it creates an enlargement of what you get in the time that Jesus reigns! Yes, it's hard to fight pride and be humble, but the reward will be amazing for those that do it!

I'll finish this section by giving you a simple formula to help you with Pride. Anything that you do successfully, immediately give Praise to God! If you take credit yourself, that is pride. If you give credit to the One Who created you, that is humility. Start here if you don't know where to start. Want another quick one that will help? When you disagree with someone, stop and realize that you don't have to be right. Stop and say "I'm sorry" if you are wrong.

Stop the argument. Sometimes, we have so much Pride that we have to be right on everything, that we will shift the argument till we are right on something! These are simple ways to start turning Pride into Humility, which gets you more of God!

Those who hunger and thirst for justice or righteousness....will be satisfied...(Matthew 5:6)

This verse in the NLT says God blesses those who hunger and thirst for justice. Other translations use the word righteousness here. The Greek word used can mean either. It really means that God blesses – Gives more of Himself – Sets apart – those who are hungry, thirsty, and have a desire to be more acceptable to God! This Greek word is really a broad term that can mean integrity, virtues, purity, or correctness in how we act.

Maybe I could simplify this by saying something like "God blesses those who strive to live a life that is pleasing and acceptable to Him". If you are learning more and more about the nature of God, what His instructions are, what Jesus tells us to do – And, if you have a desire to live out God's expectations every day as you begin to work hard to live out what you are learning, He will bless you!

It's not hard to see that the world is going the opposite direction, away from the Will of God. Every day, the world is going against more and more of His instructions, but there is a reality that some of the church is doing the same, while calling it acceptable due to the Grace of Jesus. Or, maybe some are devoted to following God's instructions, but they do it begrudgingly. Jesus is trying to tell us that we need to be passionate, hungry, thirsty to do what God expects of us!

If we live by the minimums of trying to obey God as little as possible, or we live by the world, we won't get more of God (Blessed), and we will never be satisfied. However, if we live each day more and more dedicated to God, trying to live a life more pleasing and more acceptable to Him, not only we will be Blessed – not only will we get more of Him – not only will He enlarge Himself to us – we are promised that we will be satisfied. The world will offer satisfaction, but it only lasts mere moments. Jesus is talking about a sustained satisfaction that can only come through hungering for more of God! The more you allow Jesus to transform you, the more you allow God to shape your heart, the more you live a life pleasing to Him, the more satisfied you'll be! In contrast, the more you live for the world, for success in the world, you will never be satisfied.

Those who are merciful will be shown mercy…(Matthew 5:7)

This one should be a "no brainer", but unfortunately, we live in a very broken world where Mercy is not the norm. Mercy means to help someone or to give aid to someone when it is not deserved. This is an area that we can clearly see a difference between the world and the kingdom. In the world, mercy has been lost by many. Selfish desires for money, power, position, and fame have led to a world where "selfless" people get taken advantage of, frowned upon, and often looked down on as the weak in society.

Contrast that with the Kingdom of God. EVERYTHING in the kingdom is based on Mercy. EVERYTHING! Many will look at the bible and see a God of wrath in the Old Testament, followed by a God of mercy in the New Testament. However, if you truly read both the Old and New Testament, you will see a Father, The Creator, full of mercy for those who choose Him. You'll see a God of mercy for those who turn back to Him (repentance). You'll see a God of mercy for those that go against worldly ways, while remaining obedient to Him.

Yes, He's also the Judge, who brings punishment and consequences to those that are continually disobedient, but He is full of Mercy to those who trust Him, to those who obey Him, and to those who constantly seek to please Him. We need to make sure that we stop and see that! Over and over in the Old Testament, He gives chance after chance, warning after warning, for His people to return back to Him. He doesn't force them to turn back to Him. He gives them a choice – Free Will. He warns them over and over through the prophets. Sure, there are times that we see a wrathful, judging God – but that's only after His chosen people have gone hundreds of years ignoring His warnings. Unfortunately, we often see it that way, without seeing the extreme mercy that He gave to them. When I read the Old Testament, I see an extremely patient Father that is begging His children to come back to Him – to obey Him. We have examples with stories like David, where God restores David and blesses David, as David comes back to God through a repentant and changed heart.

The promise that Jesus gives us in verse 7 is a big one. Not only do you get more of God – not only does He enlarge Himself to you if you are merciful to others, but the person who gives mercy will also be given mercy from God. It's an "if/then" statement! If you are merciful, then you will receive mercy. Maybe a better way to say this is to say – For those who are merciful to others, God will enlarge His mercy to them. For those who show mercy, God will give more of His mercy to them. That should be a huge motivation for each of us to make it a point to show mercy to others!

Those with pure hearts will see God…(Matthew 5:8)

In Chapter 3, we talked about the scripture in 1 Samuel 16, where it is made clear that God has one criteria that is important to Him – our hearts. Naturally, as humans, we tend to look at the wrong things to judge someone's success. Another way of saying this is that we tend to want to change the wrong things about ourselves to become successful by the world's standards. Often, that has to do with outward appearance. The most beautiful women in the world become models or become famous, wealthy actresses. The most handsome men become the famous wealthy actors. We tend to look at these type of people and desire to be like them. So, we'll spend countless amounts of money on gym memberships, weight loss plans, weight loss surgeries, plastic surgeries, and other things to try and achieve a better "look".

But, in scripture, it is clear that God doesn't judge a person by how they look, but by their hearts. In the story in 1 Samuel, Samuel is looking for a man to replace King Saul as the next King of Israel. Jesse, who is David's father, naturally puts his best, tallest, most handsome sons up for Samuel, expecting Samuel to pick one of them. He was expecting one of them to be picked, based on their stature or looks. David is off, tending the sheep, serving his father, but left out of the selection process. As we read these words in 1 Samuel, The LORD was rejecting the ones that had the right outer appearance to be King, because they did not have the right heart. He desired a person with the right heart. In Acts 13 verse 22, it says "²²But God removed Saul and replaced him with David, a man about whom God said, 'I have found David son of Jesse, a man after my own heart. He will do everything I want him to do.'"

That verse goes against what they saw as worldly success back over 3,000 years ago, and it goes against what we see as success in our world today. This is a clear place where Jesus is emphasizing that we need to be different from the world for Him to know us, and for us to receive God's blessing. In that scripture in Acts, we get a clear indicator of what a "God like" heart is ---- It says He will do everything I want him to do. To have the heart of God is simply to do what God says! We don't need to overcomplicate this! Do what God says = Heart of God.

It's important to point out that David was far from perfect. David made huge mistakes. Lust led him to get a married woman pregnant. That led him to have her husband, who was a faithful warrior and servant to David, killed in battle. That led to a cover up. All of it ultimately led to the death of the baby. There were consequences for the bad, sinful mistakes and decisions that David made. So, from that, we can see that failures and sin don't necessarily disqualify us from having a heart like God's. It's what David did after that when he changed, when he repented, when accepted His consequences – consequences that would haunt him the rest of his life – that's what made his heart right.

This is not a license to sin. Consequences will follow sin. It's what you do to change from that sin that helps define your heart. Your failures don't define your heart. Your repentance and obedience define your heart. We are told early on in Genesis that we are made in God's image. Part of that image is that we are given His heart. Sin, disobedience, chasing the world take us away from the heart of God that we are designed to have. But, when we are obedient, constantly looking to correct our sinful behavior, constantly making changes to try and do what God wants us and instructs us to do, that's when are hearts become Pure.

Jesus is telling us in verse 8 of Matthew 5 – when you obey God, obey His instructions, turn back to Him, that's when you see MORE OF HIM! It takes hard work every day, but look at the reward you get when you do!

Those who work for Peace…(Matthew 5:9)

This one is simple, right? Work for peace, seek peace, and you will receive more of God. Unfortunately, it's not that simple in our world. We live in a world that seems to be full of chaos, turmoil, unrest, contention, discord, trouble, crime, strife, conflicts, and wars. Sadly…it's not just the world. Often, our church environments and our families exhibit these characteristics as well.

I would argue that if I ask you to think of any area of your life that fits one of these words I just mentioned, you may be able to write me a book about the opposite of peace in most of our families, jobs, churches, country, and world. But, if I ask you to think of an area of your life that is full of peace, we often struggle to find one place.

Our enemy knows that chaos and these other things will separate us from God. How does he (satan) know this? He knows this because Jesus tells us right here that striving for peace is what gets us more of God! It's what gets us a blessing! Some translations say peacemaker, but mine says those who WORK for peace. I think that's the reality. God desires and offers peace. The world offers the opposite. To achieve peace in our world, whether we are talking about a nation or a family, it requires work. To be a peacemaker means that you are working for peace.

You CAN have peace in this crazy world, and you will get more of God when you are the one striving, working to make peace! It's easy to create chaos. It's easy to create strife. It's easy to create conflict. It's hard to create peace. But - when you do, you get more of God!

Those who are persecuted for doing right…(Matthew 5:10)

We are warned in scripture that there will come a time that "good will be called evil and evil will be called good". Isaiah warned us in Isaiah 5 verse 20. Paul warned Timothy in 2 Timothy 3 verses 1-5. I think it's safe to say that our society has reached that point more so than at any other time in history. It can get worse, but it's not likely to get better before the return of Jesus. I hope, as a follower of Christ, that we can spark a revival in our nation and in our world to turn this around for good. But, I know, through scripture, that we are facing the harsh reality that things get worse before the return of Jesus.

When we get discouraged and sad about this reality, we need to look at this verse. If you do right, you will be persecuted in a time that calls evil good and good evil. But, when you continue to do right, which means remaining obedient to God when the world turns so bad, YOU WILL GET MORE OF GOD!!!!! That's the encouragement we need to get through tough and difficult times when the world is coming against us. No one said it would be easy, but Jesus is giving us the incentive to persevere through the persecution. Jesus is giving us the incentive to get through these evil times that exist in our world.

We have reached a point in America where the name of Jesus is offensive to many. I can't understand and won't ever understand how we got here. The name of Jesus is all about peace, selflessness, love, mercy, and grace. But, in the world's eyes, all those amazing things are considered "dangerous". How are those things dangerous???? So, we have a decision to make as believers. When the world turns more and more against us and persecutes us, will we cave to the world? Will we just hide? Or, will we stand boldly for Jesus, and get more of God through our persecution that comes from obeying Him?

I think it's worth mentioning. As Americans (if you are reading this in America), we really don't know or understand what persecution is. Someone verbally attacking us on social media hurts our feelings, if we are to be honest. But, in other nations, around the world, there are Christians dying every day because of their belief in Jesus. In addition to the deaths, 1,000's are being persecuted for their belief in Jesus. My point is that we are pretty spoiled in America. For the most part, we have been a "Christian nation" since our birth 200+ years ago; therefore, we have been largely immune to true persecution. However, each day, there is a reality that we are 1 day closer to real persecution in America. Please don't let that bring fear into you. Rest knowing that you will get more of God – God will enlarge Himself to you – You will be Blessed by persevering the persecution that comes from doing what is right!

Those who are mocked, lied about, and persecuted for doing right…(Matthew 5:11-12)

Jesus ends this section of the sermon on blessings with the hardest one to grasp, in my opinion. How do you feel when people mock you? How do you feel when you've been persecuted, or realize that persecution is coming? How do you feel when people lie about you? How do you feel when people say all sorts of evil things about you? If we are honest, none of those feel good, right? Not only that, but most, if not all of them, invoke a nasty response from us as humans….even as believers.

Mock me…..I'll mock you back. Persecute me…..I'll plan a way to get you back….or at a minimum, I'll desire for your consequences to be equal to mine. Lie about me….and maybe I'll lie about you too. Say evil things about me….and I'll say evil things about you too. Maybe, on those last two, you or I won't return evil for evil, but at a minimum, we'll work hard to try and set the record straight if we've been lied about. We will wear ourselves out, defending how we aren't lying or defending how those evil things that were said about us are NOT true.

Now, we read the words of Jesus here, and He tells us that when these things happen, we get more of God. When people mock you for believing in Jesus, you get more of God! When people persecute you, as we talked about earlier, you get more of God. When people lie about you, you get more of God. When people say all sorts of evil things about you, you get more of God!!

If we read these words, and we truly believe them, then we should hope all 4 of these things are happening! People are just helping us get more of God!!!!! God promises us that He takes what the enemy means for evil, and He turns it for good (Genesis 50 verse 20). That's what Jesus is saying here. Many of the blessings that we've discussed so far have mostly to do with what we do, or how we respond, or how obedient we are. This promise of blessing happens when the world does what it does best....mocks, lies, persecutes, says evil things. Are you saying that I'll get rewarded for other people's bad behavior? Yes, that's the promise! Praise God!!

Then, Jesus steps it up in verse 12 – BE HAPPY about it! Be VERY GLAD! Up to this point, we get some cool promises – more of God – an enlargement of Him. But look at this closely. First, He says BE HAPPY – BE VERY GLAD! I don't know about you, but that goes against almost everything in me! I'm usually defensive, not happy or glad, right? But, what He says next is what we need to get our arms around. Up to this point, the reward of a promised "blessing" should be and has been encouraging, but now Jesus says ----- With this one, you get a great reward in heaven!!! There's your motivation to start changing how you feel about people coming against you. You get a reward in heaven! We should be begging for non-believers to mock us! We should be begging for people to persecute and lie and say all sorts of bad things about us! Not only does He promise rewards in heaven, He says this puts you in the company of the ancient prophets. How cool is that!!

Summing up the blessings...

This is the first part of the blueprint that Jesus gives us in a sermon that teaches us how to be known by Him. Each one has a great reward. Each one goes against the norm of the world and often against the hypocrisy of the church. Each of these is an instruction from Jesus to evaluate and possibly change how we think, how we react, and how we respond. He never said any of them would be easy, but He does say that each one gets us More of God and it gets us KNOWN BY JESUS!

By the way, many of these simply don't seem fair. Unfortunately, this walk on Earth with Jesus doesn't always seem fair. I find encouragement in remembering something simple. Jesus did NOTHING wrong. He was killed, murdered for doing nothing wrong. That doesn't make sense to me as a human that He was killed for no real reason. However, I sure am glad He took on that "unfairness" for me and for you and for anyone who believes in Him! He modeled this life for us. He modeled these blessings for us. He understands how hard it is to live a life, devoted to our Father. When you are struggling, I hope this thought helps encourage you to keep persevering. Jesus lived it, and He knows how hard each of these are for us.

My final encouragement on the blessings. Don't read this once, and be satisfied. Read this list over and over, asking the Holy Spirit to help it sink in. Read this list over and over, asking the Holy Spirit to show you the areas where you need to make changes. Read this list over and over again, asking the Holy Spirit to help you understand the rewards from each area that you change to become more aligned with these blessings. As you do this, Rest in the Peace of knowing that Jesus is getting to know you more and more as you seek to know Him more and more! And, you are getting more of God – He is enlarging Himself to you as you allow Him to change you!

Questions and Application for Chapter 4

1. What area or areas, listed out in the "blessings", do you have more of a world view than a kingdom view?
2. Are you willing to change from a world view to a kingdom view?
3. Are you more concerned with making more money, getting a better job, or getting more education than you are about pursuing the things that are important to the kingdom?
4. Which one of these (money, career, more knowledge) is the biggest struggle for you?
5. Will you shift your view of mourning/sadness to be a good thing?
6. Will you be more willing to allow others to mourn now that you understand the importance of their mourning?
7. Are you willing to look in the mirror and recognize Pride? Are you willing to work on Pride? Is Pride a problem for you? (If you aren't sure, ask someone close to you!).
8. Do you hunger to be more like God wants you to be?
9. Are you hungry for more of God, or are you satisfied with getting the minimum of God?
10. Do you show mercy to others? Do you expect mercy without giving mercy?
11. Do you have a heart that God would say is like His Heart? Do you need to make changes to have your heart more aligned with His?
12. Which is more evident in your life, chaos or peace?
13. Do you fear persecution? Will you remain faithful to Jesus when persecution comes?
14. How do you feel when you are mocked? Persecuted? Lied about? Have untrue, evil things said about you? Will you be happy about those?????
15. Challenge – Take an inventory of these areas of your life. Allow Jesus to transition your mindset from a worldly mindset to a kingdom mindset!

Prayer

"Father, First of all, THANK YOU for telling us what we can do to get more of You! Thank you that You are willing to give more of Yourself to us. Thank you for allowing us to change our hearts to be more like Your heart! Thank you that You desire to make our hearts like Yours! Thank you for laying out all the ways that we can get more of You! Please help us to evaluate each area of "the blessings". Help us to evaluate where we need to change. Help us to evaluate and change our thoughts to what You want versus what the world says is success. Please give us the strength and the courage to change our minds and actions to be more Kingdom focused, and less worldly focused. Show us the prideful areas that You want to turn into humble areas. Show us how to give more mercy to others, even when they don't deserve it. Father, give us a hunger and a thirst to know You more! Give us a hunger and a thirst for more of You! Help us to create Peace, and help that peace to overcome any chaos in our lives. And Father, help us to change our mindset when we are mocked, when we are persecuted, when we are lied about, and when all sorts of evil things are said about us. Help us to be GLAD – VERY GLAD when these things happen. Again, I simply THANK YOU for the promise that we can have more of you, as we allow you to change the way we think!!"

5

Salt and Light

Are you salty?
I want you to imagine that you are sitting down for a meal. You are very hungry. You have a plate of food in front of you that looks amazing. You take one bite, and suddenly realize that it's missing something. Maybe, it's just a little bland. What's the first thing that we typically reach for? Salt. Pass the salt please – I need a little more flavor on this meal. As I mentioned earlier, I live in the south, and I don't remember ever sitting down to a table that didn't have a salt shaker handy, no matter the meal. In fact, we have a joke with my father – I'm not sure I've ever, in my 48 years of life, seen him eat a single meal without adding more salt to it!

Salt is a universal seasoning, used all over the world. It's also used all over the world to preserve things, like meat, fish, and vegetables. I would have guessed that the United States would be the world's largest per capita (per person) user of salt. Well, I apparently didn't realize how important salt is to the world. At the time of this writing, the United States is tied for #58 on the list of salt usage around the world. There are 57 countries out there that use more salt than us? That actually surprised me.

So, what does this have to do with being known by Jesus? In Matthew 5 verse 13, we get this quick verse about salt:

"You are the salt of the earth. But what good is salt if it has lost its flavor? Can you make it salty again? It will be thrown out and trampled underfoot as worthless."

Many times, as Christ followers, we will read this verse or hear this verse, and quickly relate what Jesus is saying by comparing salt to what I shared above. If someone asks, "What does it mean to be the salt of the earth?" We can quickly give a cliché Christian answer that it means that we are supposed to be bring flavor to the world. The world without Jesus is boring…it's bland…and we as Jesus followers are supposed to make the world better, right? That's not a wrong answer, but it also not a complete answer.

As a reminder, in Chapter 4, we agreed that this sermon was being spoken to a Jewish crowd in a Jewish place. We'll explain this in more detail here in this chapter, but we need to understand that salt meant a lot more to the people that Jesus was speaking to, than simply being a flavor additive. When Jesus told His followers that they are to be the salt of the earth, it would have meant something deeper to them in their time and in their culture.

First of all, yes, we are supposed to bring flavor to those around us, whether they are believers or not! In the beginning, the world was designed to be perfect. It was paradise. Adam and Eve gave all that up for the temptation of more in the garden of Eden. The enemy tempted them with more knowledge, and they failed. In that moment, the world went from perfection to bland, so to speak. Now, Jesus is saying to the people. If you truly know Me, if you follow Me, if you obey My instructions, and if you want to be known by Me, your job is to add flavor to those around you. In a world that lacks flavor, you can bring something to that situation – to your job, to your family, to the world around you! When you bring Jesus into the room, everything suddenly "tastes" better.

In other words, as believers in Jesus, we are designed to bring something better to those around us. We are not designed to let the world bring us down. We are designed to offer something with more taste to the world! We are not designed to let the world bring us down or influence us in a negative way. We are designed to bring up those around us and influence them in a positive way.

He quickly cautions, though, that salt is no good if it's lost its flavor. It's worthless. It can't be made salty again. It will be thrown out and trampled underfoot as worthless.

When you believed in Jesus, when you made a decision to follow Jesus, when you made a decision to obey Jesus, you became salt. You have something to offer to the world. At that same time, the enemy, satan, began working hard to try and make you and me lose our flavor. He began to try and convince us that we don't have flavor. He began to try and make us believe a lie that each of us by ourselves doesn't have enough salt, as one person, to provide flavoring for the world. So, first of all, I want to make sure that we know that we have to rebuke that lie that we don't carry enough salt. I do this by saying out loud, "In Jesus name, I rebuke a lie from the enemy that I'm not enough salt to bring flavor to the world!"

Why would satan want us to think these lies? He knows the power that a little salt has. It doesn't take much salt to change the flavor. Likewise, it only takes one of us to change the atmosphere around us in a positive way. It only takes one positive person to lighten up a negative crowd. It only takes one person not having a foul mouth to help others realize they don't have to talk that way. It only takes one person not participating in gossip to begin to stop gossip. I could go on and on with examples.....

However, there is a reality that many Christians walk into a flavorless situation, at work or at home or out in the market place, and we either forget to be the salt…or we are too scared to be salt…. or we think we aren't enough salt. For whatever reason, we end up blending in with the bland instead of adding flavor to the bland. Jesus gives us a warning here about that. If the salt loses it's flavor, it's useless. This is a clear warning from Jesus. You are designed to be salt – to bring flavor – if you lose that flavor – it's worthless. That's a challenging part of that verse that we need to take to heart and to understand.

Fertilizer? The Dung Pile?

Now, let's go a little deeper into the meaning of what Jesus meant by salt. In Luke, we have a similar telling of the importance of salt, but we get a few key words that we don't see in Matthew. Luke 14 verses 34-35 says:

> [34] "Salt is good for seasoning. But if it loses its flavor, how do you make it salty again? [35] Flavorless salt is good neither for the soil nor for the manure pile. It is thrown away. Anyone with ears to hear should listen and understand!"

Salt is good for seasoning. Ok, we get that. Then, He says that flavorless salt is good for neither the soil nor the manure pile. Some translations say the dung pile. So, if flavorless salt is no good for the soil or the "poop" pile, what good is flavorful salt for either of these things?

Back in the time of Jesus, they would have relied a lot more heavily on salt than we do, using it for many more purposes than we do. They had a virtually unlimited supply of salt nearby at the Dead sea. Not only was salt useful for many things, it was relatively easy to get. If you are not familiar with the Dead Sea, it has roughly 10 times more salt in it than our normal oceans. People go to the Dead Sea as a popular tourist attraction because you can lay in the water of the Dead Sea and float with incredible buoyancy, due to the level of salt.

Yes, they would have used salt to flavor food and to preserve food, but they also used salt to fertilize crops and to stop the bacterial growth on the town's dung piles. I know it's hard for us to imagine life without modern septic systems or modern sewer systems, but back during this time, they didn't have toilets in their homes. They didn't have "outhouses" nearby. There would have been a designated place on the outskirts of town where everyone in the town or city would have gone if they had to....how do I say this politely....go "number 2". I realize that you weren't expecting a discussion about human feces in this book, but it's biblical, so please bear with me.

As you can imagine, these particular areas of the town would become pretty rancid in smell, and who knows how bad the disease and germs would be in these areas. Salt was not only a flavor additive, not only a food preservative, not only fertilizer, but it was a great way to keep down the smell, germs, and disease at the dung piles.

Now, I hope you have a better understanding of what Jesus meant in Luke when He says "Flavorless salt is good neither for the soil (fertilizer) nor the manure pile (smell and disease control).

Pass me MORE salt please...

Now, let's take this one step deeper. If you want to add flavor, you just add a small amount of salt. If you want to preserve meat, it takes more salt. If you want to help something grow, it takes even more salt. If you want to stop bad things, it takes a whole pile of salt!

They would put so much salt on a dung pile to stop the smell and to stop the spread of germs and disease, that modern archaeologists have found the remains of intact dung piles during excavation efforts in Israel. In 2017, archaeologists uncovered what they believe to be a nearly 3,000 year old military fort for King Solomon. As they excavated, human bones were found, and a very distinctive dung pile, covered and preserved in salt, was found.

What's the point? As a believer in Jesus, as a follower of Jesus, we aren't just supposed to help preserve and add flavor. We are designed to help good things grow. And, we are designed to stop bad things from growing...bad things that will harm others. Helping good things grow might be discipling an individual as they begin their relationship with Jesus. Helping good things grow might be serving at a local ministry or church. Helping good things grow might be a father becoming the spiritual leader of his home and teaching his wife and kids about Jesus. Helping good things grow might be you giving someone a word of encouragement when they need it most. I could give many more examples, but I hope you get the point. It only takes a little salt to add flavor and preserve, but it's a little harder and more intentional to disciple someone or to serve. I'll call this adding more salt.

What about examples of piling on a ton of salt to stop something bad from growing? Maybe that's what happens when you stop a "gossip" discussion from moving forward at work. Maybe that's what happens when you take the steps to drop your pride and work on a failing marriage. Maybe that's what happens when you go to your local school board meetings and demand that they don't put pornographic books in the school's library. Just like the examples of fertilizer, I could give many more examples. As you might have guessed, these are harder to do – they take more time and effort – they take more salt!

Do you have flavor or are you bland?

I gave an example earlier about how Christians can just tend to blend in to work situations, as an example. Or maybe they cave and lower their standards while in a negative environment.

Jesus doesn't endorse any of these in scripture. Now, I'm not saying that we need to walk in and start flipping tables. Remember, we just covered the importance of the peace maker in the last chapter. What I'm saying is that we are designed to bring positive things into this world. Our world is broken. It's flavorless and quite honestly, it's becoming more and more of big dung pile every day, as evil increases. We have the solution – we have the salt! We are designed to make the world around us better as followers of Jesus!

So, we add to our list. You want to be known by Jesus? Be the salt that adds flavor. Be the salt that preserves. Be the salt that invests in others and fertilizes. Be the salt that stops bad things from growing and stinking!

Are you a bright light?

The next 3 verses in Matthew 5 are verses 14-16, and Jesus expands our analogy of bringing salt to the world. He now says that we are supposed to be a light to the world! We are designed to be the salt AND the light to the world around us. He says:

> [14] "You are the light of the world—like a city on a hilltop that cannot be hidden. [15] No one lights a lamp and then puts it under a

basket. Instead, a lamp is placed on a stand, where it gives light to everyone in the house. ¹⁶ In the same way, let your good deeds shine out for all to see, so that everyone will praise your heavenly Father."

I think that Jesus is telling us with the salt and light analogies that there should be no question to the those around us about whether we are followers of Jesus or not. Have you ever met someone, talked with them for an entire conversation, and walked away with no clue whether or not they are a follower of Jesus? Flip that. What would they say about that conversation with you? Would they know that you are a Jesus follower?

As we transition to this analogy about light, we need to realize that a light can't be put out in darkness. If you are truly a light, everyone should see it.

Let me give you an example. Let's say you walk into a completely dark room at night. It's pitch black. You can't see anything at all. You can't see your hand in front of your face. What's the first thing that you think? Typically, the first thing that you think is…"I need a light". We feel for the light switch on the wall, or maybe we have a flash light nearby, or maybe we grab our cell phone and turn on its flashlight feature. The point is that we just want some light in there, right? It's so natural for us to desire light in a dark room, that we instinctively turn on a light switch in a dark room, even when the power is out! We all do it!

Once you turn on a light of any type, now, light is showing through that darkness. Darkness can't exist when the light is on. You can't have half light and half darkness. You either have complete darkness OR you have some type of light that pierces that darkness. Some lights are brighter than others, but even the dimmest flashlight or the dimmest candle provides light in a dark room.

It's up to you how bright you want to be….

It's the same for us in the world. The world, as a whole, is a dark place. The world has a lot of darkness in it. But, when a Jesus follower shows up in that place, we are supposed to carry a light that makes total darkness unachievable in that place.

I didn't say that everyone there was going to like or appreciate your light. There is a reality that certain people may work hard to try and put out your light. At this point, I'm just trying to get the point across that you carry the Light of Jesus in you as a follower of Jesus, and you are supposed to be a light that pierces through darkness. If someone can carry on a conversation for 30 minutes with us, and then walk away from that conversation not knowing if we are a Jesus follower or not, I'd say it's safe to say that we forgot to turn on our "light switch".

Many Jesus followers look like salt and light while they are at church. Church is a safe place. But, as soon as they leave that parking lot after church, it becomes hard to distinguish believers in Jesus from non-believers. Is that what Jesus asks of us? Go to church, be the best Christian you can be for the hour or two you are there, then head on back out into the world and be darkness. NO, of course not! He says that your light is supposed to be like a city on a hilltop that can NOT be hidden.

If you are in a dark wilderness, and you are searching for a place to go when you're lost, you may see a light far off in the distance, and at least you have a place to go toward when you are lost. Well, the world is no different. Some people are lost, and they are ok with being lost. They will stay dark. However, some are lost and they are searching. If we are being a light, like a city on a hill, at least they will know about you, see you, and maybe they can make their way toward you to find light! Jesus says no one lights a lamp and then puts in under a basket. The lamp is placed out where it provides light for the whole house.

So, how do we make sure our light is shining? I'm glad you asked – because our Savior Jesus loves us so much that He gave us the answer in verse 16! You want to be a light? Let your good deeds SHINE out for all to see, so that everyone will praise your Heavenly Father!

We know that we are saved by the FREE grace of Jesus's shed blood. That's a grace that we can't earn. However, we also know from scripture that we prove our faith with GOOD WORKS. Back in Chapter 1, we discussed James chapter 2 verse 19 where it said

"You say you have faith, for you believe that there is one God. Good for you! Even the demons believe this, and they tremble in terror."

Now, let's look at the next verse. James 2 verse 20:

"How foolish! Can't you see that faith without good deeds is useless?"

Now, look at verse 26:

"Just as the body is dead without breath, so also faith is dead without good works."

When someone "believes" in Jesus, we will say that they have faith in Jesus. James says congratulations, you are equal with demons when you believe in Jesus. Now, your faith and belief is useless and dead without good works or good deeds. James is pretty clear in helping us understand that it's not true faith to simply believe. Our faith is proven or shown by our good works. And Jesus says here in Matthew 5 that you show your light by letting your good deeds shine for all to see.

What I'm hoping that you are getting is that showing up and being the salt and light at church or at a Christian concert or at a Christian event is not what James or Jesus is talking about. They are talking about doing your good deeds out in a broken world. The good news about our broken world is that you don't have to look far to see opportunities to be salt and light. You can be these things at a restaurant, at the gas station, at your work, at your child's ballfields, at the golf course, with your non-believing family at the holidays, or at your home – daily for each of these! I could obviously list off many more examples, but I hope that you are getting the point.

Church services, Christian concerts, and other Christian events are great things. Those are the places that we go to get refreshed, re-energized, and encouraged to go out to be salt and light in a dark, tasteless world that is full of piles of dung. Jesus said be salt to the world….be a light to the world….let your good deeds shine in the world. Church needs to be a place where we can be honest with our hurts and pains. It needs to be a place where like-minded, loving people rally around us to prop us up. It needs to be a place where we are encouraged. It needs to be a place where we get prayed over. It needs to be a place where we get filled with the Holy Spirit. Why?? So, that we can go back out to the nasty, dark, tasteless world, and be the flavor, be the preservative, be the fertilizer, be the "stopper" of bad things, and be a light that draws others out of darkness with our good deeds, done for everyone to see!

Jesus is telling us that we have a purpose as His follower. We aren't just believers in Jesus for what we get out of it. He expects us to take our belief in Him and do something with that belief. As we do, we have to be careful that we are giving ALL praise to the Father. Jesus is clear about that as well. It's not about what I can do or what you can do as a follower of Jesus. It's about what He allows us to do as His followers to bring His love, hope, and salvation to a broken world.

Coming up in this sermon, we'll see a time where Jesus tells us not to brag about our good deeds and our giving and our prayer time, so I want to go ahead and address this now. He's not contradicting Himself. Later, in Chapter 6, He'll be addressing those that do these good things with the wrong heart. Here in Chapter 5, He's telling us what expectation He has for us, and He expects it to be done with the right "heart". If you are bragging about what you do, you are bringing glory to yourself. Jesus wants us to do these good things and let them shine out for the world to see AS WE GIVE CREDIT AND PRAISE TO THE FATHER!

Jesus's hope and goal is for everyone to come to Him. In verse 16, it says "so that everyone will praise your heavenly Father." His desire is that everyone will come to Him. I once heard a pastor say something profound. He said Hell was designed for satan and his evil angels…not humans. Our Father offered His Son Jesus to be crucified for ALL. Jesus wants us to be a Light so that EVERYONE would come to Him!

Time to evaluate…..

When we read this, sometimes, it can feel overwhelming. We might feel motivated, but then we might get bogged down in overthinking and overcomplicating the impact that we can have. I want to give a simple example of how simple this can be.

Most people that know and follow Jesus have a testimony to share. At some point in our lives, we have been broken. Maybe we knew Jesus during this time. Maybe we didn't know Jesus yet. Either way, Jesus helped us out of a bad situation. Now, when you meet a broken person, simply tell them your story. Tell them how you were broken, and how Jesus saved you from that situation! Your story might be the simple HOPE that they need to have the courage to change or to have the courage to keep going. You may not think you have much to offer, but by sharing, you are being salt and light!

Did you know that God will put people in your path that He wants you to help? Do you believe that? If you didn't know that or you don't believe that, I want to help you change your mind. For me, I trust God to put men in my path that have struggled with the same things that I have struggled with. I have a testimony that is too long to tell here in this book that includes alcohol addiction, rejection, pride, sexual sin, and a whole list of other issues.

Constantly, I meet men struggling with one or more areas that is a part of my testimony. As they share their problems and burdens with me, I begin to share my testimony back with them. I talk openly about my failures, followed by how Jesus saved me from that life and how He has restored me to a point where I can help others in the same situation. Don't let the enemy try to tell you that you have nothing to offer someone. Don't let the enemy tell you that it's not safe to share your story. Sharing your story – your testimony is powerful and can be a great help to someone in a time of need. Revelation 12:11 says "They triumphed over him by the blood of the Lamb and by the word of their testimony". This is talking about satan's defeat by two things – The blood of Jesus AND the word of our testimony. You never know what God can and will do with your story, in terms of using it to help someone.

As we evaluate this, we have to be honest with ourselves. We don't want to let the enemy beat us up, making us believe lies that we have nothing to share or nothing to offer. But, at the same time, we have to be honest with evaluating what kind of impact we are having as Jesus followers. Is my home better because of my faith in Jesus? Is my work environment better because of my faith in Jesus? Is my child's sports team that I'm coaching better because of my faith in Jesus? Is my spouse better because of my faith in Jesus? Are my friends better because of my faith in Jesus?

Jesus is asking us to self-evaluate on each of these things He's teaching us. Each environment that we are in might need a different level of salt. Each environment may need a different level of brightness out of our light. The good news is that we don't have to be perfect in any of this. All Jesus is asking us to do is try. As you work on these things, it gets easier, and you get better at what you are offering. This involves a level of faith and trust in the Holy Spirit to guide you to the right amount of salt, and the right amount of light that a situation needs. If you try your best and mess up, you'll learn. Jesus's Grace will catch you and support you. Don't give up. Learn from your mistakes, get up, and do it again. Trust the Holy Spirit to help you.

Good list vs the bad list.....

I have one more place I'd like to go in scripture to help us evaluate if we are bringing salt and light to the environments around us. In Galatians 5, we have a famous scripture about the "fruits of the Spirit". Paul lists out the aspects of our lives that people should see in us if we are dedicated followers of Jesus. Before he gives that good list, he gives us a bad list – a list to stay away from. I'm sharing this for a reason that I will explain.

Galatians 5 verses 19-23:

[19] When you follow the desires of your sinful nature, the results are very clear: sexual immorality, impurity, lustful pleasures, [20] idolatry, sorcery, hostility, quarreling, jealousy, outbursts of anger, selfish ambition, dissension, division, [21] envy, drunkenness, wild parties, and other sins like these. Let me tell you again, as I have before, that anyone living that sort of life will not inherit the Kingdom of God.

[22] But the Holy Spirit produces this kind of fruit in our lives: love, joy, peace, patience, kindness, goodness, faithfulness, [23] gentleness, and self-control.

We have the "bad list" in verses 19-21. Then, we have the "good list" in verses 22-23. One way to evaluate where we are is to take an inventory for each list. As a warning, this may hurt a little…this may be a little difficult.

How many of the items from the bad list do I have? How many items from the good list do I have? We need to be honest as we evaluate. After we evaluate HONESTLY, our goal is to stop doing the things in the bad list, and to produce more of the things in the good list. The hardest part is the self-evaluation.

I preached this in a sermon over two years ago. There was a lady in our congregation that came to us very broken, and I'll use the word "worldly". She was raised as a believer. She had a foundation of faith in Jesus. But, her life was producing much of the bad list and little of the good list. That's the bad news. Here's the good news. She was hungry to grow. She was hungry to know Jesus more. She was hungry to be known by Jesus.

She began to evaluate each day by how much of her day fell into the bad list verses the good list. It became something that we talked about. One week, she would say, "I'm still living in the bad list a lot, but I'm starting to see a few in the good list". My wife and I watched her literally evaluate everything in her life, family, and career, comparing which list it fell under. Over the next year and to now, I have watched the Grace of Jesus change her life. Jesus has changed every aspect of her life, for the positive. I didn't say she doesn't still struggle from time to time. We all struggle at times, and I believe we will until we meet Jesus. But, she self-evaluated EVERY aspect of her life. As a result, I watched her love for Jesus and her love for people grow to the point that she is SALT AND LIGHT every day for many people now. My wife and I tried our best to be the salt and light she needed. Now, she is reaching people that we don't have access to, which is amazing! It's been a beautiful thing to watch. It's been one of the most encouraging things I've ever experienced as a pastor. That's why I wanted to include that example in this book. She self-evaluated, and she made changes. I don't know if Jesus knew her 3 or 4 or 5 years ago, but I know Jesus knows her now!! Her light is shining bright, and she is using each aspect of the salt analogy!

So, if you don't know where to start evaluating if you are salt and light, start here with these two lists. It's pretty easy to see which list you are living out of – if you simply evaluate your actions. No matter where you are in your journey, I think it's important that we always self-evaluate through this list. Then, be ready to share what Jesus has done to bring you out of darkness.

You want to be known by Jesus? Change the atmosphere for those around you. Be the salt that adds flavor. Be the salt that preserves. Be the salt that helps healthy things grow. Be the salt that stops bad things from growing. Be a light in a dark place. Share your story about Jesus. Evaluate where you stand on the good/bad list. Make changes as the Holy Spirit reveals the "bad" areas to you.

Whatever you do, please, please don't lose your flavor, and please don't hide your light under a blanket!

Questions and Application for Chapter 5
1. Do you add "flavor" to those around you? If not, what do you need to change to add flavor?
2. Do you help "preserve" the good things about Jesus by helping others know these things? (For example, if none of us ever tell anyone knew about Jesus, the gospel would not be preserved the way it should be. God will never allow the story of Jesus to die, but it's important for each of us to realize our part in preserving the gospel!).
3. Are you "fertilizing" by discipling anyone? If not, who is someone that you can help?
4. Are you stopping bad things from growing? What is an area at your work or home where you can help stop something bad?
5. Are people attracted to your light (Jesus), or are you hiding your light under a blanket?
6. Have you ever shared any part of your testimony? If no, Will you now? What is holding you back?
7. Which list does your life reflect more - The good list or the bad list?
8. Challenge – Be intentional about letting your light shine for Jesus. Don't be ashamed or bashful about what you can offer the world! Share your testimony with someone to give them hope!

Prayer
"Father, help me to be the salt and light You want! Help me to bring flavor to the world. Help me to preserve Your gospel about Jesus. Help me to fertilize and help others learn more about You. Help me to be a part of stopping bad things. Help me to have the courage to be all 4 of these aspects of salt. Father, help me to shine my light for all the world to see. Help people to be attracted to me to learn more about you. Help them see my light from far away, and to be attracted to my light in this dark world. Help me to know how much salt to sprinkle. Help me to know how much light to shine. Father, I thank you for taking a broken person like me, and redeeming me to the point that I can use my story – my testimony to help others find hope and to help others find your Salvation! Please give me the

courage to share my testimony. Please give me the wisdom of how much to share with each person – for what they need at that moment. Father, help me to get out of that bad list and live only in the good list! Please show me the areas where I need to change. I want to be Your salt and Your light. I want to bring Hope to a broken world. I want to live in the Fruits of the Spirit!"

6

The Law...

Don't misunderstand...
We are going to spend some time on the next verse that Jesus gives us in this teaching. Verse 17 of Matthew 5 says:

> "Don't misunderstand why I have come. I did not come to abolish the law of Moses or the writings of the prophets. No, I came to accomplish their purpose."

You may also be familiar with translations that say "fulfill" instead of "accomplish". What if I told you that we have a lot of words mistranslated in this simple, small verse? What if I told you that this is one of the most misunderstood and mistaught scriptures in all the New Testament? As we process through this, I'm asking you to be patient as I explain this. I'm asking you to be open-minded to what Jesus is telling us. This may simply be a little deeper than you've ever been taught. Or, this may seem to go against what you've been taught. Please bear with me, and formulate your opinions after I have fully explained.

He starts the verse with the statement "Don't misunderstand why I have come." That statement should grab our attention. That means that He knew that some did misunderstand AND/OR He knew that some would probably misunderstand at some point.

Let's break down some words into the Greek and Hebrew. Matthew was first written in Hebrew to a Hebrew (Jewish) crowd. It was then translated to Greek. Then, it was translated into Latin. Then, it was finally translated into English, where you can find many different English translations. I think I forgot the Aramaic in there somewhere! I'm not trying to be perfect on how many translations, but I am trying to make a point about the opportunities for mistranslation. If you look on Biblegateway.com, which is a popular online resource to look up scripture, you will find 63 different options for translations in English. 63!

The issue is that going from language to language to language to language often leads to unintentional changes in the words and meanings. That's why it is important that we go back to the Greek and to the Hebrew, if possible, to get the original meaning. I will do my best to explain this to you without it becoming a Greek and Hebrew lesson that goes so deep that it's hard to understand.

We have a word that we are familiar with in the bible, and that word is Law. Often, we hear it referred to as the Law of Moses, or the Law given to Moses, as it's written here in Matthew 5, verse 17. What do you think of when you hear the word "Law"? Usually, the word "Law" invokes negative thoughts in our rebellious hearts, if we are to be completely honest. For example, if the speed limit is 55, that's a Law for that particular place on that highway. I must confess that I'm guilty of breaking laws like this often! When I see a speed limit sign of 55, I immediately think "I can go 60 or 64 and probably not receive a ticket." I'm trying to give a simple example that most of us can relate to. Technically, I have broken the law if I go over 55, right? I justify it by thinking this is a silly law. I know it's safe to go faster on that road. At least, that's what I think. I also know through experience that most officers will not give me a ticket if I'm only going 5 MPH over the speed limit. So, in this case, I take a law, that was designed by my authority, and I redefine what I think it should be because of my thoughts and experiences. Then, if I get pulled over and receive a ticket for going 60, who do

I get mad at? Do I blame myself, the one that is guilty? Most often, NO, I am mad at the officer. I'm certainly not advocating that anyone who reads this should ever break the laws of your city, county, or state. I'm just being honest about something that most of us do every day without even caring about breaking that law. Hang on to this example as I process through this conversation and explanation.

First, let's look at the Hebrew word that God gives us, that we have translated to the word Law or often to the word Commandments. The Hebrew word is Mitzvah, which means an "instruction". In English, we translate it to "God's Law" or to "God's commandments", but it more accurately means "God's instructions".

In Deuteronomy 7:9 for example, the NLT says "Understand, therefore, that the LORD your God is indeed God. He is the faithful God who keeps his covenant for a thousand generations and lavishes his unfailing love on those who love him and obey his commands."

This tells us that God lavishes his unfailing love on these who love Him and obey His Mitzvah's – His instructions. Let's look at this with all 3 words we've discussed:

1. God lavishes his unfailing love on those who love Him, and obey His **instructions.**
2. God lavishes his unfailing love on those who love Him, and obey His **commandments.**
3. God lavishes his unfailing love on those who love Him, and obey His **laws.**

Which of these do you like the best? To me, law sounds harsh. Maybe you don't feel that way, but I'm just being honest with the feeling that I get when I hear that word. Commandment is a little softer. I prefer that over Law. Then, we have this word "instruction". It's not so much that "instruction" is softer, but when I hear that word, it invokes more of a curiosity to know that "instruction" versus a rebellious thought to oppose a "law". I'm not saying that it's up to us to pick and choose what words or verses are softer for us. What I'm saying is that if we look at the real translation, as we should, it is actually a softer word that is easier to get our arms around.

I'm much more open to an instruction that you want to give me, than I am to a law you want me to follow. You may not feel the same way as me about these words, but I hope you get my point. Each time, we hear the word "Law" or the word "Commandment" in scripture, I'm hoping you'll replace those with the true word there, which means "Instruction".

Many Christians are taught today that the Old Testament is not relative. Throw it away. They will say Jesus came to replace the Law. This is such a bad statement! It's an unbiblical statement, that is unfortunately taught in our churches every Sunday. We need to understand the true meaning and educate others that have been misled. If they argue with you or choose to stay stuck in the wrong belief because it was the tradition that they were taught, I would get away from them. That's how serious this is. Jesus did not come to replace God's instructions!

In Chapter 1 of this book, we took the time to establish that Jesus was there at creation (actually before as we discussed), and THROUGH Him all things were created. That means that God's "instructions" or Law to Moses was created through Jesus. So, Jesus creates the original instructions, and then He came a few thousand years later to do away with His own instructions? That simply doesn't make sense, and it creates confusion and false beliefs for why Jesus came. That's why I spent time in Chapter 1 to explain that He was there when God gave these instructions to Moses, because it's a crucial point to be able to understand what Jesus is saying here in Matthew 5 verse 17.

Jesus came to accomplish or fulfill

Jesus says "Don't misunderstand why I have come. I did not come to abolish the "instructions" that I helped create! I came to accomplish or fulfill. Ok, it's time for some more Greek and Hebrew lessons. The Greek word for "abolish" is "kataluo". This word means to dissolve, to destroy, to demolish, to subvert, to overthrow, or to halt. Put any of those phrases into this sentence where the blank is. "I did not come to _____ the instructions of God." I did not come to dissolve, to destroy, to demolish, to subvert, to overthrow, or to halt the instructions of God. This word is used 3 mores times in Matthew (Matthew 24:2; Matthew 26:61; and Matthew 27:40); and all 3 times is referring to the tearing down of or destruction of a physical structure. Jesus is using a word that they understood to mean "I didn't come to tear down the instructions of God."

Now, let's look at the Greek and Hebrew words that we have translated to "Fulfill" or "Accomplish". The Greek word is "pleroo", and it means to make full, to fill up, to cause God's will to be obeyed as it should. So, let's keep building on the true meaning of what Jesus was saying here: "I did not come to tear down the instructions of God. No, I came to make God's instructions full, to fill them up, to cause God's will to be obeyed as it should." If we look at the Hebrew meaning, it means to "make them louder". If we insert that meaning, we can better understand the meaning of the phrase to be: "I did not come to tear down the instructions of God. No, I came to make God's instructions full, to fill them up, to cause God's will to be obeyed as it should, to make His instructions louder!"

I stated in Chapter 1, and I'll state it again – Jesus is the only human that has ever walked the Earth that fully understands the instructions of God. He's the only human that has ever walked the Earth that fully understands the Will of God. He helped create ALL of it with the Father. Jesus is telling us that part of His purpose is to fully convey to us, to fully teach us, what God's instructions mean. God's instructions were laid out to humans, and even the best scholars started trying to figure out the deeper meaning of the instructions. Then, over centuries, men have put their own parameters around what God meant.

Fenced in....

I've heard it explained this way. God put up a security fence to protect His people. It was NOT intended to punish them. It was NOT intended to restrict them from good or fun things. It was designed to PROTECT them from the evil of the enemy. Then, man tries to make sure he understands the borders of the fence. The problem here is that no man (other than Jesus) truly understands the boundaries of the fence. So, to make sure that man doesn't get outside of

God's fence, man puts up a smaller fence inside God's fence. We don't understand God's boundaries, so let's put up a smaller fence inside God's fence, so that we make sure we don't cross God's boundary. This mentality creates "religion". This mentality creates "rules-based" love with God. This mentality creates restrictions to the relationship that God intended and desires to have with us. It creates man-made religion. Even done with the best intentions, it creates traditions that we call biblical – that simply may not be biblical.

Now, Jesus comes along, and says – "Hey! I know where the fence boundaries are! I'll show you. I'm the only HUMAN that truly knows the boundaries. I helped create them. I know what the Father wants!"

This is huge to understand and get our arms around. If we look at Jesus as a replacement of the Law, which is what many Christ followers are taught, it's simply false. It becomes what some will call a "replacement theology". But, if we take the time to look at this for what God intended, it actually widens our knowledge of the Father, and will help deepen our relationship with Him.

Now, instead of throwing away the Old Testament, or instead of looking at it as a set of rules that condemn me, I can see the greater picture of the Heart of the Father. Let's look at Deuteronomy 7:9 again. Maybe you've dismissed a scripture like this one because you were taught that Jesus did away with the Law. If He did away with the Law, why would I read and care about Deuteronomy 7:9?? But now, through a better understanding of the purpose of Jesus, I read Deuteronomy 7:9 in a different way:

"Understand that the LORD your God is indeed God. He is the faithful God who keeps His covenant (promises) for a thousand generations and lavishes His unfailing love on those who love Him and obey His instructions."

What a beautiful verse that we may have been missing out on! He is God!! He is faithful!! He keeps His promises!! He lavishes unfailing love on those who love Him and obey His instructions!!! This opens my eyes more and more to the promises that I can receive by my faith in Jesus!! This helps me understand how YOU and I get His unfailing love!!! Who wouldn't want God's unfailing love?

I know this was a deep dive, but I hope you now have a better understanding of why Jesus came. I hope this helps you understand that the Old Testament is still important for us as believers today. He came to help us better understand what the instructions from the Father are expected to be. We'll get great examples of this when we get to verses 21-48 in Matthew 5, where Jesus talks about anger, adultery, and a few other topics. He'll continue to explain what it means to "fully preach" or "fill it up". I'll go ahead and give you a spoiler alert. Many men have interpreted God's instructions to be about the physical things that we do. Jesus will fully preach God's instructions by taking it deeper to the heart. Physical action leads to religion and traditions. The heart leads to being known by Jesus!

Till heaven and earth disappear...

If you've read this far, and you immediately jump to a conclusion that I'm saying that all of God's instructions from the Old Testament to the New Testament remained the same, please know that is not what I'm saying. For the purpose of this book, I'm hitting the high points to help you understand what Jesus means in Matthew 5, but this is not intended to be a deep study on what instructions apply to us as Gentiles versus what instructions were for the Hebrew people only. I hope this gives you a desire to know more and to dig deeper.

There are some instructions that were for the Israelites in the land of Israel only, for example. I'm not an Israelite in the land of Israel; so, not all of the instructions apply to me. We are not expected to perform animal sacrifices today. Scripture is clear that Jesus was sacrificed as the Lamb – once and for all – to take away my sins. This discussion is about finding the balance and not being hypocritical.

Man, I hate hypocrisy...

I want to give a few examples of what I mean by hypocrisy. I've heard many Christians say that Jesus did away with the Law. But, then, they talk about keeping the "ten commandments". Isn't that hypocritical? To say "Jesus did away with the Law, but I still keep the Ten Commandments that sum up the Law" is a hypocritical thought or belief. He either did away with them or not.

I've also heard many Christians say that Jesus did away with the Law, but then they say it's a sin to get a tattoo. So, I'll ask – "Where does it say that we should not get a tattoo?" To which they answer – "It tells us not to get a tattoo in Leviticus 19:28." So, which is it? Can we get a tattoo or not? You told me that Jesus did away with the Law, but then you referenced the Law to say it's a sin. That's hypocrisy, and quite honestly, it drives me nuts to hear things like this. Last time I checked, Jesus had a lot to say about hypocrisy and how we need to NOT BE HYPOCRITES! We'll get there here in a few chapters...

That's why this discussion is important. As Christians, we often don't even realize what we are saying, and how hypocritical it is. Let me give you another example of why it's important to understand this. Paul and Jesus talk about sexual sin in the New Testament, right? In 1 Corinthians 6:18, Paul says "Flee from sexual sin!" Coming up here in Matthew 5, Jesus will talk about adultery. Where is sexual sin defined, including adultery? It's defined in Leviticus 18 – in the Law – in the instructions. Why didn't Paul explain what sexual sin was to these Gentiles before saying to "flee from sexual sin"? Why didn't Jesus explain what adultery was to these Hebrew people (and possibly Gentiles) before He talked about adultery? They didn't have to define it because it was a part of God's instructions that were taught! Same today, if I tell you not to commit sexual sin. Where would I send you to understand what sexual sin is? You guessed it! I would send you to Leviticus 18. Good thing we didn't throw away all the Law....or all of God's instructions on sexual sin! I'm sorry if this sounds like I'm being a bit sarcastic, but I really can't stand hypocrisy and doublemindedness, yet our teachings on this are full of it. If we don't sort this out properly and accurately, IT WILL AFFECT HOW WELL YOU ARE KNOWN!

Religion...Greazy Grace...

Several pages ago, I gave you the example of me driving over the speed limit because I've decided to we-write that instruction or that law to better suit my desire for that moment. That's sort of what we are doing as Christians. We take the parts of the bible that we like, and then we discard or we-write the parts of the bible that we don't like – to better suit our desires for that moment.

Before Jesus, they took the instructions and made a fence within a fence, so to speak. They made God's instructions harder than they had to be – out of devotion to make sure they didn't change an instruction. 2,000 years later, we tend to look down on those people as "religious", while we soften many of God's instructions, because Jesus's grace covers all sin, right? For those people 2,000 years ago, Jesus was saying "let me better explain what God meant with that instruction." For us, it's the same thing! I think He would say, "I didn't die so that you could do anything you wanted and get away with it because I died for it…..because I shed My blood for it….".

His message SHOULD be equally important to us, as it would have been for the religious people of His time. The religious leaders of the Old Testament often put up a fence within a fence – to make sure they didn't approach that outer fence of God's instructions. They wanted to make sure they didn't cross over. That, as we have stated, creates "religion". Now, 2,000 years later, we tend to put up our fences OUTSIDE of God's original fence. We think we know better, and He didn't really require us to obey all His instructions…. so, let's put up a fence outside His fence. Now, we cross over His boundaries daily and rely on the Grace of Jesus to cover it. That creates what I will call "greazy grace". Neither extreme (religion or greazy grace) is good! That's why Jesus is telling us that He came to explain correctly! Thank you Jesus!

Details matter…

In verse 18 of Matthew 5, Jesus says "I tell you the truth, until heaven and earth disappear, not even the smallest detail of God's law will disappear until its purpose is achieved." Have heaven and earth disappeared? Obviously, the answer is NO! So, God's instructions won't be totally complete until that time, unless the purpose for that instruction has been achieved.

Let's give a few examples. God's instructions told the people how, when, and why to make animal sacrifices at the Temple to

God. After Jesus's death, burial, and resurrection, we as believers don't have to make those sacrifices anymore. Why? The purpose for the animal sacrifice has been achieved. It was achieved when Jesus became the ultimate sacrifice for us with His death, burial, and resurrection. He was the ultimate sacrificed Lamb!

Now, let's go to an opposite example. God's instructions tell us to not participate in sexual sin, as we just discussed. Paul reinforces those instructions. Jesus reinforces those instructions. This is an instruction that will not disappear until heaven and earth disappear. Sexual sin will plague this world as we know it until Paradise is created with the New Heaven and the New Earth (Revelation 21), where there is no more sin.

As I write this, I don't claim to know or understand the status on each of the instructions from the "Law of Moses"; however, now that my eyes have been opened, I'm trying my best to learn more and make changes where needed. It's not a performance based, works based, "law" based mentality. It's a principle based on my love for the Father and my desire to please Him, to obey Him, so that I get MORE of Him! I want to be lavished with His unfailing love. That's the motivation to continue to learn more each day.

Again, my purpose is not to break down all 613 instructions given in the "Law of Moses" and tell you which ones apply today versus which ones have had their purpose achieved. My goal is to open our eyes to the fact that even caring about this, knowing the truth about this, and researching this will help each of us get closer to God. This desire to know more and understand Him more is a great step to being known by Him!

A jot or a tittle…

Before we leave verse 18, I want to point out one interesting fact. Hopefully, none of us are changing the word of God. In verse 18, my translation (NLT) says, "not even the smallest detail of God's law will disappear until its purpose is achieved." Another translation (NIV) says "not the smallest letter, not the least stroke of a pen". Another translation (KJV) says "not one jot or one tittle". Let's explain this and tell you why it matters. The Hebrew language is very complex. A letter in Hebrew can also be a number. It can also be a word. It can also be a phrase. We often don't get a one-to-one word translation from Hebrew to English. That's why we often go back to the Hebrew text to get a more complete or more full meaning. You can take a letter in Hebrew and change one mark to the side of the letter, and it completely changes the meaning. Remember, the Old Testament, and the instructions were written in Hebrew.

There is a very important prayer in Hebrew, called the "Shema". For centuries, this prayer has been a "centerpiece" to the prayers that would be prayed daily by God's people.

There is a Hebrew letter or phrase that says "Here is our God". You can take that, change one "jot or tittle", which is sort of like this symbol for us – ' – and it changes the meaning from "Here is our God" to "Is there a God?" See the importance now of not changing one thing?! What's more is that it still pronounces the same. So, you can take this prayer, it sounds the same, but changing one small written part, changes the meaning from "Here is our God" to "Is there a God?" Wow, I don't want to pray that one the wrong way!

One more example. Mark Biltz is a great teacher and author that I greatly respect. I have been blessed to learn a lot more about the depth of scripture through his teachings and books. God has gifted him! I highly recommend a book that he wrote called, "Decoding the Antichrist and the End Times: What the Bible says and What the Future Holds". It's an incredible resource to go deeper into this area that we've covered in this chapter.

In his book, Mark details out how Solomon changed his Torah – his instructions – his copy of the Law to suit his needs. I'm going to give a quick summary to make a point, but please purchase and read his book for a better, deeper understanding.

It's important to know that they didn't have printing presses like we have today. So, back when a man was crowned King of Israel, he would have his own Torah handwritten. The more you understand about the importance of the stroke of a pen, the more you will understand how long this would take, and how precise it needed to be.

In Deuteronomy 17, starting in verse 14, God's instructions (His Torah) lay out "guidelines for the king". There are three areas that

Mark talks about in his book, mentioned in this scripture. The king will not build up a large stable of horses (verse 16). The king must not take many wives for himself (verse 17). The king must not accumulate large amounts of silver and gold (verse 17). Verse 18 says "When he sits on the throne as king, he must copy for himself this body of instruction on a scroll in the presence of the Levitical priests."

Well, what do we know about King Solomon. He multiplied his horses, his wives, and his gold and silver. The instructions say don't do it. Solomon did all 3. When he wrote his version of the Torah, even though it was in the presence of the priests, he made a few small tweaks….he changed a jot or a tittle. Instead of saying a king must NOT multiply his horses, wives, and gold, he wrote a king must multiply his horses, wives, and gold. There was a reason that God told the king not to multiply – we'll just take wives as an example. Because Solomon had wives he should have never had, it corrupted him. Let's look at 1 Kings 11 verses 1-6:

"Now King Solomon loved many foreign women. Besides Pharaoh's daughter, he married women from Moab, Ammon, Edom, Sidon, and from among the Hittites. ² The LORD had clearly instructed the people of Israel, "You must not marry them, because they will turn your hearts to their gods." Yet Solomon insisted on loving them anyway. ³ He had 700 wives of royal birth and 300 concubines. And in fact, they did turn his heart away from the LORD.

⁴ In Solomon's old age, they turned his heart to worship other gods instead of being completely faithful to the LORD his God, as his father, David, had been. ⁵ Solomon worshiped Ashtoreth, the goddess of the Sidonians, and Molech, the detestable god of the Ammonites. ⁶ In this way, Solomon did what was evil in the LORD's sight; he refused to follow the LORD completely, as his father, David, had done."

Solomon changed a lot with a jot!
Solomon changed a "jot" or a "tittle", and it led him to turn his heart from God. He even turned to the point that he sacrificed his own children to Molech!

This is why it's important that we truly understand what scripture says and what it means. God's instructions have been given to us to protect us, so that our hearts don't turn away from God. God is not trying to restrict our fun, or our freedoms. His instructions are given completely out of love, to protect us, and to keep us away from the evil, antichrist spirit that is in the world.

I'm passionate about this. When a Christ follower says that Jesus came and did away with the law, it makes me sad to see how misled they have become. Why would God send the Messiah to save us, while simultaneously taking away His instructions that protect us? Does that make sense? No....it doesn't.

We can't change even the smallest thing in scripture to make it say what we want it to say, or to make it fit our agenda. We have to learn and submit to God's instructions, given for our protection, to keep our hearts turned toward Him!

The famed preacher and theologian, Martin Luther, who helped lead the "Protestant Reformation" and lived in the 15th/16th century, once said, "The Law (instructions) is not necessary to justification (salvation), but it must be kept in the church to reveal sin, to maintain discipline, and to advise Christians what is pleasing to God".

I'll restate this in 21st century terms. Jesus offers the free gift of salvation (justification) that we don't deserve. We still need God's instructions to know right from wrong, and to know how to please God.

The least in the kingdom....

Ok, back to the Sermon on the Mount. Raise your hand if you want to be the "least in the kingdom of God". Hopefully, NO ONE raised their hand. I doubt that any of us want to be the least in the kingdom. Don't get me wrong. Ultimately, I just want to be in the Kingdom. But, let's be honest, I don't want to squeak into the Kingdom as the least!

In verse 19, Jesus says "So if you ignore the least commandment and teach others to do the same, you will be called the least in the Kingdom of Heaven. But anyone who obeys God's laws and teaches them will be called great in the Kingdom of Heaven."

If we say that Jesus came to do away with God's commandments – His Torah – His Mitzvah's – His Law – we are doing the very thing that Jesus describes as the thing that gets you called the Least in the Kingdom. I guess the good news is that He doesn't say we'd be excluded from the kingdom. However, He is clear – if you ignore ONE of God's commandments and you teach others to do the same, you will be called the least in the kingdom.

This may be the incentive we need to go on a lifelong journey to better understand which instructions (laws) still apply, and which ones don't. Some still apply. Don't murder – still applies. Don't lie – still applies. Animal sacrifices – does not apply since Jesus shed His blood. Those are just a few easy examples.

Jesus gives us a choice here in this scripture. Ignore the least instruction and teach others to do the same, you will be called the least in the Kingdom of Heaven. BUT, anyone who obeys God's instructions and teaches those instructions will be called GREAT in the Kingdom of Heaven. Given those two choices, I choose Great! How about you?

The minimums....

Now, as you've read this chapter, maybe you still want to argue. Maybe you are confused. After all, in Acts 15, it says Gentile believers don't have to do any of that law stuff, right? Well, let's go read it.

Acts 15, verse 1:
"While Paul and Barnabas were at Antioch of Syria, some men from Judea arrived and began to teach the believers: "Unless you are circumcised as required by the law of Moses, you cannot be saved."

So, we have a scenario where Jewish believers in Jesus are telling Gentile believers in Jesus that they must be circumcised, as the Law of Moses states, in order to be saved. They were incorrectly telling the new Gentile believers that it took an action on their part – a work, so to speak – to be saved.

Then, in verse 5, it says:

"But then some of the believers who belonged to the sect of the Pharisees stood up and insisted, "The Gentile converts must be circumcised and required to follow the law of Moses."

Now, the Jewish believers are trying to tell Gentile believers that they must be circumcised and required to follow the law of Moses. Remember, some of the "laws" are for Jews in the land. The Jewish believers were trying to put all their requirements onto the Gentile believers.

Then, in verses 19-20 – it says:

[19] "And so my judgment is that we should not make it difficult for the Gentiles who are turning to God. [20] Instead, we should write and tell them to abstain from eating food offered to idols, from sexual immorality, from eating the meat of strangled animals, and from consuming blood."

Now, we have the leaders of the church (the Jesus following church), getting together to figure out what the Gentiles had to do as a minimum. James, the leader of the church, is talking here in verse 19, when he says it will be too difficult to make the Gentiles do everything that we do as Jews. He is essentially saying….We've been doing all this since birth, so it's second nature to us. It's all new to the Gentiles and may overwhelm them. So, let's make it easy on them and tell them to stay away from eating food offered to idols, stay away from sexual immorality, stay away from eating the meat of strangled animals, and stay away from consuming blood.

James and the early church leaders got together and came up with "minimums" for the Gentile believers. The key word there is minimums. Here's a question I have for you. And, it's a question I've asked myself. Do you want to meet Jesus – who suffered a horrible death and sacrificed His life for you to be with the Father forever – and tell Him that you did the minimums for Him?

"Hey Jesus! Thank you for dying for me! That was incredibly awesome! To thank you, I did the bare minimums for You…"That is not where I want to be in the conversation with Jesus when I meet Him!

There is a difference between what you Have to do and what you Can do. There are your minimums. That's enough, but you are at least expected to do those. What's ironic and hypocritical is that some Christians will read all this, not make the connections that I'm trying to make, and tell me that they don't have to do anything but believe. But, we are told in scripture that to believe means to obey. We are told that to show God and Jesus that we love them, that we need to obey. So, I find it hypocritical that many in the church today are welcoming sexual sin into the church through homosexuality and transgender identities, clearly defying and disobeying a minimum, while calling me super religious because I have a desire to have my heart turned more toward Jesus.

Let's give an example about adoption…

I want to give an analogy that I use often to help explain this. It's an example, so please bear with me. By ethnicity, I'm a white, male, American. I was born into a white, American family and raised by that family. But, for the sake of an example, let's say I was born American, but adopted by a Chinese family. That family is ethnically different than me, but they don't make me perform their customs. They have committed to provide shelter, food, and safety for me till I'm 18. But, they don't make me learn Mandarin. They don't make me use chopsticks to eat. They don't make me wear a Hanfu (traditional Chinese robe for men). They don't make me celebrate the Chinese New Year with them. They allow me to be 100% American, and they don't force their Chinese traditions onto me.

They do, however, have some ground rules that I MUST follow. Let's make these easy. I can't cuss, drink alcohol, or do drugs in their house. I'm just trying to make up a few easy things to understand. I don't have to follow all their traditions, but I am required to meet some minimum "rules".

Then, over time, as I mature, I become more thankful for them adopting me when they didn't have to. I grow to love them more and more. Now, I decide that I'd like to learn some Mandarin. I don't have to, but I can. And it would honor them. I decide that I'd like to learn to eat with chopsticks. I don't have to, but I can. And it would honor them. I decide that I'd like to wear a Hanfu and attend their Chinese New Year celebration. Once again, I don't have to, but I can. And it would honor them. As I take on their traditions, or at least try, it would show them how appreciative I am, how much I love them, and it would greatly honor them.

Now, let's take this example to a Jewish versus Gentile discussion. I'm 100% Gentile. I decide that I'd like to learn some Hebrew. I don't have to, but I can. And it would honor our Father. I decide that I'd like to learn more about the Jewish customs. I don't have to, but I can. And it would honor our Father. I decide that I'd like to wear tassels like Jesus did and celebrate the Jewish festivals. Once again, I don't have to, but I can. And it would honor our Father.

For example, our church has chosen to sing a few songs each week in Hebrew, as well as in English. We have decided to celebrate each of the Jewish festivals (Passover, Rosh Hashanah, and Sukkot for example. There are more…just trying to give examples). We don't have to…we aren't trying to be more Holy than another church….but, we can do this to Love and Honor Our Father.

As we take on these Jewish traditions, or at least as we try, it shows our Father how appreciative we are and how much we love Him for adopting us into that "tree" that we weren't supposed to be a part of. Again, we don't have to, but we want to. Why? This devotion to Him gets us turned more toward His heart, and less toward the evil of the world. The more you turn toward His heart, the more He will know you!

There are some minimums that I have to do – some rules that I'm expected to follow, right? Doing more is my choice, and if I choose to do those things to honor our Father, why would anyone disagree? You might think I'm a little cooky for doing it, but please don't tell me it's "wrong". It may be optional, but it is not wrong.

At least do the minimums!

Those leaders set the minimums for the Gentiles. Most of those minimums aren't a problem for us in America. We don't usually have to worry about abstaining from food offered to idols, or from eating the meat of strangled animals, or from consuming blood. I do have a story where I was offered "fried duck blood" once, but you get my point – we don't see these 3 things often in our culture.

But, what about that 4th one – sexual immorality? Do you think it's not prevalent in the church today? Forget for a moment what I mentioned about homosexuality and transgender being justified in some churches. I know stories of pastors who have committed adultery with their assistants for example. It has ruined families and churches. In my own church, a lady once tried to convince us and the church that God would be ok with her sleeping with another man outside of her marriage because it would make her happy. Wouldn't God want her to be happy, she asked??

What about pornography in the church? What about pastors that are addicted to pornography? I read a study that found that 68% of church-going men view porn on a regular basis. Over 50% of pastors view porn regularly. When you look at young Christian males (18-24 years old), it jumps to 76%! What about women? It stated that 87% of Christian women have watched porn at least once? It stated that 56% of American divorces involve one party having an "obsessive interest" in pornographic websites.

This is what happens when we set up our fences of greazy grace outside the fence of God's instructions. We start to allow and justify that the church doesn't even have to meet the minimums. And, then, we wonder why the church is declining and weak in America.

So, if we aren't going to go above the minimums, which we can, we at least need to DO THE MINIMUMS!!

A warning....

As we close out this chapter, I want to quickly look at verse 20 of Matthew 5. Jesus gives a warning. Whenever Jesus warns, it would be good to PAY ATTENTION!

> "But I warn you—unless your righteousness is better than the righteousness of the teachers of religious law and the Pharisees, you will never enter the Kingdom of Heaven!"

As believers, we can tend to get lazy...complacent...and rely on a greazy grace from Jesus that is not biblical. We can start to develop the mentality that "I'll do whatever pleases me, and Jesus grace will cover it." Well, Jesus gives a warning here that is quite the opposite.

We tend to look down on the Pharisees and the leaders of religious law of the time of Jesus, right? The fact that we believe in Jesus makes us better than all of them, right???

In the scripture that we just covered in Acts, it references Pharisees (more than one) who were believers in Jesus (Acts 15 verse 5). Did you catch that when we read that verse? We tend to associate the term Pharisee with a bad religious person that doesn't believe in Jesus. That's actually an unfair and incorrect stereotype that we are often taught.

Jesus's warning says that our righteousness has to be better than the righteousness of the Pharisees – if we want to enter the Kingdom of Heaven. Wait! I thought that being a Jesus believer was an easy road – an easy path – simply believe – and go to heaven and live happily ever after? Is it not?

Jesus is clear. He expects us to be righteous. The Greek word here is "dikaiosyne", which means to attain a state that is acceptable to God. It can also mean a correctness of thinking, feeling, and acting. What Jesus is saying is that I expect you to get to know me more and more. I expect you to learn more and more about the Father's instructions that He expects for your life. I expect you to DO SOMETHING! Not just learn, but change your Heart and actions to obey the Will of God.

Jesus has been clear in these verses (17-20). I want to make sure you know why I've come – my Father's instructions are very important – and I expect you to do something with what you know!

This chapter has been intense. This chapter is one that may take some time to comprehend and dig into. But, as you allow Jesus to correct what you've been taught, and as you allow Him to teach you the instructions of His Father/Our Father, you can rest knowing that you are attaining righteousness, which grants you entrance to the Kingdom of Heaven, where you will be known by Jesus!

Questions and Application for Chapter 6
1. Do you feel like you have a better understanding of why it is important that we don't throw away the Old Testament?
2. Does this make you want to learn more about God's instructions that can benefit your life?
3. Do you have a better understanding of why Jesus came?
4. Does using the word "instruction" make it easier on you to be obedient?
5. Do you have any conflicting hypocritical beliefs that need to be evaluated?
6. Have you ever lived too far into the "Religion" category OR too far in the "Greazy Grace" category?
7. Are you ok with being the least in the kingdom, or do you want more?
8. Are you ok with meeting Jesus and telling Him you just did the minimum to get there?
9. Challenge – Make a decision to start living your life to the "maximum" of obedience to Jesus. Don't settle for the minimums!

Prayer
"Father, thank you for ALL of your instructions. Thank you that you love us so much that you gave instructions to protect us! Father, please help me find the balance of what you need me to understand out of this chapter. Please help me to see and learn your Word in its completeness, and not to get lazy or complacent in just knowing what I need to get by. Please expose the hypocrisy in what we are taught – so that we can have a hunger to learn the truth. Please help me find the perfect balance of learning and obeying your instructions, while relying on the Grace of Jesus when I fail. Please help me not to get "religious", and please help me not to rely on "greazy grace", but to find Your Heart, which is the perfect balance!"

7

oh...no...Jesus actually makes it harder...as He fully preaches it...

Anger is murder...
As believers in Jesus, we have traditionally been taught that Jesus came, He died, He arose, He ascended to Heaven to be with the Father, and His blood covers our failures and sins. That's all correct. That's all very scriptural and VERY important. But, then, we say things like "good thing we don't have to follow the Law anymore..... that was too hard." Well, in this chapter, we're going to focus on the reality that when Jesus came, He actually made some things harder. If you remember from the previous chapter, He came to fully preach God's instructions. He came to "preach it up". He came to make it LOUDER. We are about to see exactly what this means.

As I've said before, the Law of Moses (the instructions given to Moses) are mostly about your outward actions. Jesus then comes to fully explain the "instructions" and tells us that obedience and disobedience to those instructions starts with the Heart, or maybe we would say it starts with our thoughts.

In Matthew 5, verses 21 and 22, Jesus takes an instruction from the Law of Moses and makes it harder. He says:

[21] "You have heard that our ancestors were told, 'You must not murder. If you commit murder, you are subject to judgment.' [22] But I say, if you are even angry with someone, you are subject to judgment! If you call someone an idiot, you are in danger of being brought before the court. And if you curse someone, you are in danger of the fires of hell."

Jesus is very clear. The "Law" (the instructions) says do not commit the physical act of murder, but I say, if you are even angry with someone, it's the same as murder. Do you see what I mean when I say He made it harder? Now, I'm really thankful that His blood is there to cover my sins, because I can't count the # of times that I've been angry with people in my life.

With the Law of Moses, it was about the physical act of murder. You and I could be angry with someone, call them an idiot, and curse them, but as long as we didn't physically murder them, no sin had taken place. Now, Jesus says, I'm stepping it up! If you are angry, you have sinned. If you call them an idiot, you are in danger of the sin. If you curse them, you are in danger of hell!

Under the Law, I'm innocent! I haven't murdered anyone! Under Jesus's "preached up" explanation of what God meant, I'm very guilty because I have often been angry with people. Thank you Jesus that your sacrifice is there!!

So, God gives the instructions, the mitzvah's, the Law to Moses. It is taught for many generations not to do the physical act. Now, Jesus comes along as the only human who fully understands the intent of those instructions, given to Moses, and He tells us that the intent goes deeper than the physical action. It's about the thought. It's about your heart.

It says "if we call someone an idiot" or "if we curse someone". If we look at the Greek words here, idiot is the word "raka", which means senseless or empty headed. That's pretty much what it means when we say idiot in English. But, when we look at the word curse, it is the Greek word "moros", which is best translated to the word fool. It's were we get the English word moron. So, Jesus is telling us that calling someone an idiot….a fool…a moron can be just as bad as murdering them! Again, as I've stated, Jesus has made this harder, but that's not the point. He is really telling us that the Father expects us to not be angry, and to be careful how we think and talk of others.

When I first read this, I realized that I was "murdering a lot of people". As I just stated, I have never physically murdered someone, but I was guilty daily or weekly of doing it "in my heart". So, I had to begin to work on that thought, because I want to be closer to Jesus, and I want to be closer to what the Father expects and wants of me. I'm not perfect on this, but I've gotten better with not getting angry as easily as I would have in the past. I think we have to be careful that we allow ourselves the grace to work on these areas AS the Father exposes them to us. Once it's been made aware to us, we need to work on it, understanding better what the Father expects of us, but we also have to be patient with ourselves as we learn a completely new and different thought process!

To be completely transparent, the part of this that I struggle with the most is what I say about people. It can be as simple as someone cutting me off in traffic. I don't get angry and chase them down to fight (like I used to), but I quickly call them an idiot! I quickly call them a moron! My point is that I think we need to be constantly self-evaluating where we need to work on being a better follower of the instructions that Jesus has given to us. The Law says "Don't Murder". Jesus says "Don't Be Angry" and "Don't call them an idiot, a moron, or a fool". You and I might be working on these till the day we die, but each day that we are trying to correct our thoughts, is a day that we are getting closer to Jesus!

Learning to take the thought captive…

Part of being known by Jesus is understanding that God cares just as much about us cleaning up our thoughts as He does about us cleaning up our actions. In 2 Corinthians 10 verse 5, Paul says:

"We destroy every proud obstacle that keeps people from knowing God. We capture their rebellious thoughts and teach them to obey Christ."

The NLT says "capture their rebellious thoughts". You may be more familiar with what the NIV says – "we take captive every thought". Let's break this down into a simple format. A thought comes into your head. I am going to argue that the thought itself is not a sin. Now, I'm supposed to analyze that thought. Does this thought line up with scripture or is it disobedient to scripture? If it lines up with scripture, I can now act on it or say it. Everything is fine. But, if that thought does not line up with scripture and if that thought is disobedient to scripture, then I'm supposed to capture that thought and teach it to obey Christ. I am not free to act on it or say it.

Step 1 is analyzing the thought before doing anything at all with it. Step 2 is comparing it to scripture. Step 3 is either acting on it or taking it captive, based on how it lined up with scripture.

Let's give a few examples to make this clear. This first example will have a choice of good or bad, maybe I should say multiple choices. Let's say that we meet a widow, who needs help. Without even trying to think, the first thought in my head is "should we help her?" 1 Timothy 5 tells us in great detail when to help widows and when not to help. I'll let you go study that passage of scripture on your own, if you would like. So, now, let's say that she meets the criteria for being helped, so I get excited to help her. At this point, my thought lines up with scripture, and we help her. That's good!

However, what if I evaluate that she is a worthy widow, but my thought is that I really don't want to help her? Now, I have to realize that my thought has become rebellious, and I have to teach it to obey Jesus. Jesus's word clearly says that I should help her, so I repent (change my mind), and we help her. This ends in a good way, but I had to take a rebellious thought captive, a thought that did not line up with scripture, and make that thought become obedient.

For this to happen, we have to be continuously learning scripture, we have to be willing to evaluate how our thoughts and actions line up against scripture, and we have to be willing to make changes when our thoughts and actions don't line up with scripture. The humility it takes to do this will be rewarded by Jesus, no matter what the subject or thought started out to be. His Grace will be there to cover that rebellious thought, and I'm so thankful for that! He is not asking us to be perfect. He is the only human that was perfect or could be perfect. He is expecting us to evaluate and change to be more like Him.

Now, let's look at another example that some of us encounter daily. Maybe I'm getting old....and maybe this is something that old people say....but I swear....people are getting crazier every day in terms of driving!

When I was 18 years old, someone cut me off in traffic. I sped up and followed them to the next red light that caused us both to stop. I got out of my truck, ran up to the car, and tried to open the door to fight the man inside. He locked the doors....he looked terrified....and I think this just fueled my fire. I beat on the windows, and eventually kicked a dent in his door.

I'm not proud at all of this moment, but sadly, this was a time in my life when I declared Jesus as my savior. This was a time in my life that I claimed to be His follower. Did any of my thoughts or actions prove that? Did any of my thoughts or actions line up to scripture? Obviously, that would be NO to both questions. By the way, the entire time that this was unfolding, I was calling him a bunch of words and names that were much worse than idiot, moron, or fool!

Let's fast forward to about age 30. A man cuts me off in traffic, and this time, I have a wife and small child in the car. This made my anger spiral out of control, at the thought of either of them getting hurt because of this "idiot's" driving. My anger raged, and I honestly think I was ready to kill him. I chased him to a parking lot, where we cussed each other up and down. Now, this is a problem. Thinking I was protecting my wife and child, I was actually putting all of us in more potential harm.

Then, I read these words of Jesus. I realized that the anger in my heart, the words out of my mouth, and the actions that ensued are all totally against scripture. All of it was completely against what our Father wants. Today, another 18 years later, I still struggle with getting really frustrated if I'm cut off in traffic. When someone cuts me off in traffic, my first thought is often not a good thought. BUT ----- BUT ----- now, I stop and take that thought captive. I might be literally thinking "Obey Jesus…obey Jesus…obey Jesus you rebellious thought". I'm literally telling that thought to obey Jesus. As I give this to Jesus, now, I pray for that person and for the safety of those that could be impacted by their crazy driving.

I am the one who has to take the thought captive. I'm the one that has to teach it to obey Jesus. And, over time, I've noticed that my first thought is not nearly as intense and hateful as it used to be. To be honest, it's not anger that I struggle with anymore. My biggest unbiblical thought is what I want to say about them to my family in the car. One day, I simply said, "What an idiot…" Then, I hear a 9-year-old voice from the back seat say "Dad, Jesus says don't call people idiots!" That was both a proud moment for me that my son knew that, as well as a convicting thought that I have some more areas to work on! You want to be humbled? Allow your children to evaluate your hypocrisy!

I shared these examples with you to make it clear that we are all humans, and our first thought is usually slanted toward evil. In Genesis 8 verse 21, it says:

"The LORD smelled the pleasing aroma and said in his heart: "Never again will I curse the ground because of humans, even though every inclination of the human heart is evil from childhood."

This is just after the flood. Noah has survived the flood, and he has come out of the ark. God has punished the wickedness of the world and makes a promise to Noah (and to us) that He'll never flood the Earth again. But there is a key phrase there – "even though every inclination of the human heart is evil from childhood".

There is a fact that our thoughts and actions are bent towards evil; therefore, it will be a daily battle to take those thoughts captive, and to make the changes that Jesus tells us to make. I can't just conquer anger once and be done. I have to be ready every day to conquer anger. But, as we do this, we are being more and more obedient to what God intended with His instructions. As we do this, it does get easier as our hearts change to be more aligned with the Father's heart.

Most people that know me now have a hard time seeing me as an angry person now. You can pretty much walk up to me, slap me in the face, and I'll feel sorry for you...I'll give you the benefit of the doubt that you are having a bad day! I give Jesus the glory and praise for shaping my angry heart into a more loving heart. I still have areas to improve, but I've come along way. You can too!

The fear pendulum...

Before we move on to the next verses to cover, I want to give you a practical and biblical approach that I have used to deal with my own anger. I have also been blessed to have helped many people with similar issues. I'd like to tell you that the two examples I gave were my only two outbursts of anger in my life. You have probably guessed that I had a bigger struggle with anger – and I struggled a lot!

Through my journey to become more like Jesus, to be more obedient to His Word, and to make the necessary changes, I've been privileged to meet with and counsel hundreds of people. Often, these people are broken people, who are trying their best to follow Jesus, but just can't find breakthrough in certain areas.

One of the strengths that God has given me is the ability to see patterns. An easy what to say this is that most people are struggling with similar things. My job is to see the pattern that has developed and recommend help for that pattern. I thank God for this gift.

Over a ten-year period or so, I've noticed a pattern that I call the Fear Pendulum. A pendulum swings from side to side. Think about holding a pocket watch. Let's say that you are holding the chain of the watch, allowing the weight of the watch to hang freely. Now, if you begin to swing that watch, it will swing equally in each direction, due to the laws of physics. Now, we're going to take this thought, and apply it to how Fear works. I know you are probably questioning…how did we jump from anger to fear so fast? Please give me a few minutes to explain, and I will tie it all together.

First, we will start this discussion with the FACT that God does not want us to have fear. In 2 Timothy 1 verse 7, Paul tells Timothy:

"For God has not given us a spirit of fear and timidity, but of power, love, and self-discipline."

Timothy was in a place where persecution was so bad, that he was struggling with fear. People were dying all around Timothy, because of their faith in Jesus. When Timothy wrote to Paul, it is stated that many of Timothy's letters were stained with tears, due to the anguish and reality of the difficulty of being a follower of Jesus during that time.

God doesn't want us to have fear, but I will argue that one of the enemy's #1 tools is fear. Even in the garden, satan tempted Eve with the one thing she didn't have. Instead of being satisfied with all the perfect, wonderful things that she did have, satan was trying to invoke a fear into her mind that God was holding something back from her. That fear began to create doubt, and Eve failed.... followed by Adam. If satan started his attack on humans with fear as a weapon, and he used it as a significant tool against the early believers like Timothy, why would he stop using it against us today?

At the center line of the fear pendulum, we have a simple line, labeled fear:

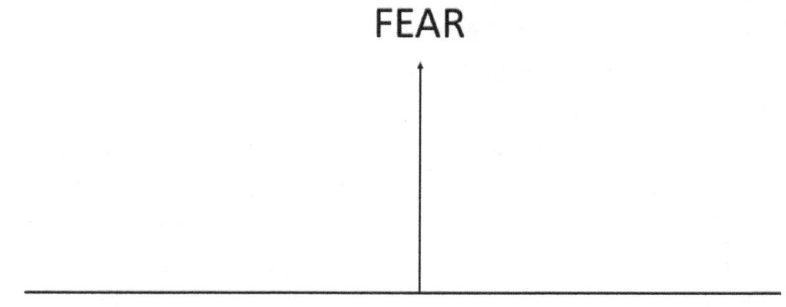

When a fear hits us, it will generally swing one way or the other. If it goes one way, we see Control. In other words, I develop a fear, and now I try to control that fear. Or, it will swing the other way, where we will try to run or hide or recluse from that fear. I either try to CONTROL the fear, or I ISOLATE or run from the fear.

To be clear, I'm not talking about a physical fear where you "fight or flight". I'm talking about a fear that comes into our minds. For example, if I have a fear that I will not be liked, that's what I call Rejection or a fear of Rejection. If that fear hits me, I will usually either recluse myself away from others (isolate), or I will try to control the situation to make you like me.

If I recluse, I'm not giving you the chance to dislike me...(which is still sort of like control). If I try to control what you think about me, I may go overboard, trying to get you to like me, or I may change my standards and do things I wouldn't normally do to make you like me. In either case, I may push you farther away, thus bringing the fear to a reality. As you can see with this simple example, it is creating a bit of chaos and strife, as the fear begins to "manifest" into actions.

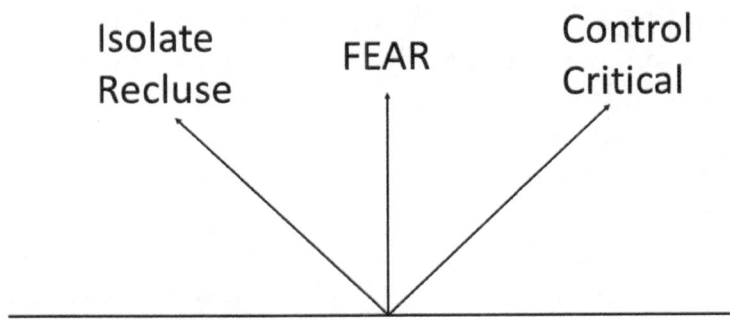

If you can control your fear, it makes you feel like that fear is gone. Or, if you run from that fear, you can pretend it's not there. But, what happens when you can't control the fear? What happens when the fear chases you?

If you can't control the fear, it leads to anger. On the other side of the pendulum – If you can't run from the fear, you'll recluse more and more till you hit a state of depression from the isolation.

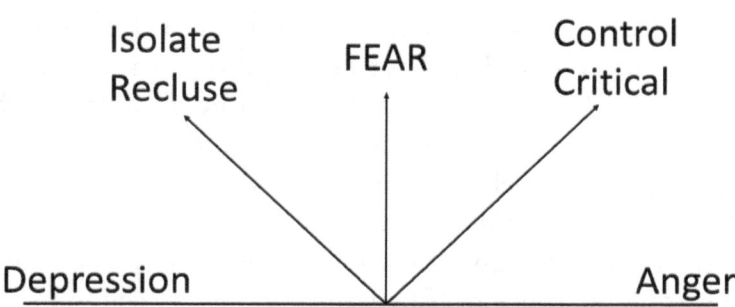

I call this a pendulum because one fear can have you swinging from side to side, from control to isolation, from anger to depression, and it becomes a chaotic thing that we call anxiety. It can become an out-of-control pendulum.

Let's give a few examples to further explain. Let's say that a fear hits, and I try to control it. If I can control it, now, I'm a "control freak". If someone is constantly trying to control their fears, you might label that person as being "OCD". Now, if you can't control your fear, you become angry. Some people pretty much bypass control and go straight to anger. Some might get stuck on control and never get to anger.

Another "side effect" that you might see is someone becoming critical. You'll see I added it to the picture above with control because being critical is often just someone trying to control something. If I have a fear about what people will think about your style of teaching for example, I can't change or control the way you teach, but I can be critical of how you teach, in the hopes that you will change. That's still a method of control....

Let's look at the other side. A fear hits, and I recluse or isolate myself. Maybe that works, but I start to feel lonely. If I stay isolated too long, it becomes depression. As with the right side of the pendulum, the fear may be so impactful that I go straight to depression.

Here's where it really gets tricky. Let's say I go from fear to anger. Then, I feel bad for what I've done or thought or acted on, and then I snap back to the other side of depression or severe isolation. Or, let's say that I go from fear to depression. Then, I can easily snap over to anger.

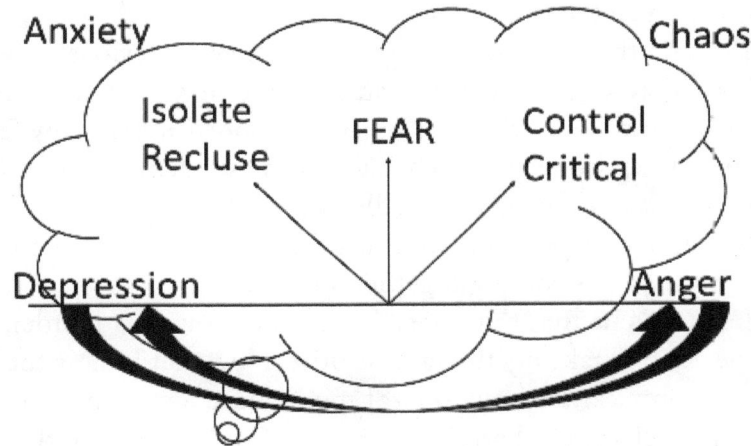

It becomes a vicious cycle that many of us experience daily. In fact, I don't recall one time that this analogy has not resonated with someone that I'm counseling. The world says take some pills and numb out the effects of this chaos and anxiety. My hope in explaining this is to give you hope that you can go to Jesus for help!

Let me apply this to my example of anger. When I feel angry, I don't try to evaluate why I'm mad. I don't try to ask God why I'm mad. I go back to the source. My prayer is simply "Father, what is the fear that led to my anger?" If I feel like a control freak, "Father, what is the fear that is driving my desire to control?" If I notice that I've become critical, "Father, what is the fear that is driving my critical nature (or desire to control)?" If I feel like I'm reclusing or isolating from others – "Father, what is my fear?" If I feel like I'm depressed – "Father, what is my fear?". If I feel like I have anxiety – "What is my fear?"

Are you getting the point? Fear drives all these unhealthy emotions that we accept daily. We might say "That's just how I am…". Well, that's not what Jesus intended you to be like, AND YOU CAN HAVE FREEDOM FROM THESE THINGS! Over and over, we read in scripture that Jesus came to "save" us. The Greek word used is "sozo", and it means much more than to save. It means to save, to heal, and to deliver. Jesus came to save you, to heal you, and to deliver you from your fear, control, criticalness, anger, depression, anxiety, and chaos!

Let's tie this back to my anger stories that I previously shared. Let's say that someone cuts me off in traffic, and I get angry. Now, I stop and ask God, "what is my fear?" He shows me that my fear is that my family came close to being in a car accident, and that accident could lead to being hurt badly or it could lead to death. I can't control how that person drives, so I went straight to anger. Make sense now? Is this coming together for you?

Jesus tells us that this anger I have is the same as murder, so I have learned to take my thoughts captive. Now that I know the true issue or root, I know how to fight more effectively. I know how to pray more effectively. I ask God what my fear is. I bind up that fear in Jesus's name. I pray for that person. Now, my heart is changed, and I'm closer to Jesus. Or, I can keep just being angry, because "that's who I am…"

One gets you closer to Jesus; the other gets you closer to hell. If I can change, you can too! If I can use this simple pendulum to help me take my thoughts captive, you can too! If I can teach my disobedient thoughts to obey Jesus, you can too! As we do this, we are getting closer to the heart of the Father, and we are getting more and more known by Jesus!!! The more you try to take your thoughts captive, the easier it becomes. The more you self-reflect, the easier it becomes to be humble and change.

Most fear and worry is irrational…

In case my anger stories don't resonate with you, I want to give you another example. I'll use a fictional example, but it's one that I see lived out often in real life.

There's a young lady, and let's say she's in a church environment. She becomes concerned that a group of people don't like her. Her husband asks why she thinks that. She tells him that no one talks to her. However, when you look at the situation, you notice that when that young lady enters the room, she recluses herself away from people. Then, she gets caught staring at people with an awkward, judgmental look. She never engages anyone in conversation.

In her head, she has a fear that no one likes her. Now, her fear is manifesting outwardly by changing her actions towards those people. She's self-protecting, isolating from people, and becoming critical in her head about the people that "don't like her".

What's the result? No one wants to be around her because she is rude and judgmental. In her mind, she's thinking, "I was right! No one likes me." The reality is that she was well liked until her actions created the very thing she was scared about to begin with. Her irrational fear caused her to change her actions, resulting in the very thing that she was fearful of in the first place! The problem is that no one ever tells her it was her fear manifesting….and the cycle continues.

Whether you are looking at this example of rejection or my examples of anger, the same thing is happening. Irrational fears have led to actions with consequences. The consequences often end up being the very thing we were scared of, but now brought full circle by our actions. Do you see why this is so important to understand and learn to change? Do you see why it causes chaos and anxiety?

We live in a time where fear is at an all-time high, in society and in churches. Pastors are reporting a 70% increase in fear since 2020. These fears include fears of sickness, fears about wars, fears about political unrest, and fears about the economy, just to name a few.

satan wants to wear us out with fear, because he knows it's an effective tool that he has against us. Fear leads to anger that leads to the equivalent of murder. satan wants to destroy us as believers, and he often does it with fear that causes us many extended problems, when we simply aren't understanding that the fear is coming from him, our enemy.

Sound mind...

I want to help you understand that this is not only to help you get rid of your anger, but also to help you get rid of fear in general. We already covered 2 Timothy 1:7, but let's revisit that verse quickly. Paul tells Timothy that God has given us a sound mind, or self-control, or self-discipline (depending on your translation). All of these things are about the mind. When we talk about irrational fears, we are mostly talking about what happens between our ears – in our minds!

I have seen a sign that says "I know worrying works, because 99% of what I worry about never happens." I can't think of a better analogy to explain this concept. Every day, we "worry", and most of what we worry about never happens because it was an irrational fear to begin with!

God intends us to have a sound mind, not one full of worry or irrational fears. So, how do we fight this? I want to look at one more quick scripture, and then we'll start tying some things together to teach you how to fight fear. In 1 John 4:18, it says:

"Such love has no fear, because perfect love expels all fear. If we are afraid, it is for fear of punishment, and this shows that we have not fully experienced His perfect love."

That's the NLT translation. If we go to the NKJV translation, it is similar, but worth noting the difference:

"There is no fear in love; but perfect love casts out fear, because fear involves torment. But he who fears has not been made perfect in love."

Let's break this down. God is Perfect Love. His perfect love casts out fear. Fear includes torment. The Greek word used there for torment means punishment.

When we allow fear to enter our minds, it pushes out God's love, AND we are punishing ourselves! God never intended us to have fear. He didn't give us a spirit of fear, and His perfect love casts out fear. satan uses fear to torment, but God gave us a sound mind that is not designed to be tormented! As you can see, this is a battle between God and satan for our minds!

So, here's a practical and biblical way to fight this. First, we have to take the thought captive. If that thought is a fear, we know immediately that it goes against scripture. Now, we have to teach that disobedient fearful thought to obey Christ!

Here's my prayer tying all this together:

"I bind up a spirit of fear in Jesus's name and tell it to leave me now! Father, your Word says that you didn't give me a spirit of fear. Your Word also tells me that your Perfect Love casts out fear. Father, Your Word tells me that you give me a spirit of Power, Love, and a Sound Mind, free of the torment of Fear, so I'm asking you to fill me with your Perfect Love to the point that fear can no longer exist!"

This an example of a prayer that you can say over and over to fight off fear and worry. You have to take the thought captive (realizing it's not from God), and apply the truth of scripture to that thought (to teach it to obey Jesus).

Fear and worry become a negative snowball that spiral into control, anger, isolation, depression, anxiety, criticalness, and chaos. These thoughts punish us by tormenting us.

Praying this prayer and retraining your mind to not accept fear and worry will have a positive snowball. As you retrain your mind to reject fear, you are less likely to act with anger, and that will help Jesus know you better!!

What about the "Good fear"???

As I've taught this concept over the years, I will often get two questions. Both really stem out of this question – "What about the good fears. Jason"?

I will then ask – "what do you consider good fear when the bible clearly states that God doesn't want us to have fear"?

First, I have a fear that my stove will burn me. Isn't that a good fear? The answer is – knowing that your stove will burn you is not fear...that is knowledge and wisdom. At some point in your past, you either got burned by a stove, or you watched someone get burned by a stove, or you just trust what someone has told you about how a stove can burn you. You don't tremble in terror in front of your stove, but you do have knowledge and wisdom that you shouldn't touch it.

Second, doesn't the bible say that we should Fear God? That's a good fear, right? What if I told you that question has a "yes" and "no" answer?

Let's take a scripture for example. Proverbs 9:10 says:

The fear of the Lord is the beginning of wisdom,
and knowledge of the Holy One is understanding.

The Hebrew word used there is "yir'a", which means "to stand in awe of"....."to respect"..."to have extreme reverence". It's where we get our modern-day word "awesome". So, let's plug those into that scripture:

"To stand in awe of the Lord is the beginning of wisdom and knowledge."

"To respect the Lord is the beginning of wisdom and knowledge."

"To have extreme reverence for the Lord is the beginning of wisdom and knowledge."

Our Father does not want you to be scared of Him. He wants you to have extreme reverence for Him, He wants you to have extreme respect for Him, and He wants you to stand in complete awe of Him!! He's AWESOME!!!

If you don't respect, revere, and stand in awe of Him, then maybe you should be in fear (terror) of Him.... See? It's a "yes" and "no" answer!

Questions and Application for Chapter 7
1. Has anger ever been an issue for you? Is it still? Do you feel better equipped to work on your anger?
2. Will you think twice now about calling someone an idiot? Or a moron? Or a fool?
3. Does the Fear Pendulum help you understand issues that you may have with Control, Anger, Isolation, Depression, or Anxiety?
4. Which one of these do you struggle with the most?
5. Will you pray against fear and bind it up, now that you know it's a problem?
6. Do you stand in awe of God? In complete reverence? In complete respect?
7. Challenge – Use the prayer and method listed out in this chapter to actively fight your fears, along with the other negative things that fear drives.

Prayer
"Father, thank you for opening my eyes to the danger of anger. Thank you for opening my eyes to the danger of me calling people degrading names. Father, help me to learn how to take my thoughts captive so that I can better teach fear to obey you! Help me to bind up fear and get it out of my life. Father, please fill me with your perfect love that casts out fear and torment. Thank you for the promise of Power, Love, and a Sound Mind. Today, I declare that my mind is being renewed to reject fear and all the negative and sinful things that tag along with fear! Father, I stand in awe of how mighty You are!"

8

still harder...

Lust is adultery...

As we continue to process through the Sermon on the Mount, we see Jesus reinforce what we have discussed in the last two chapters – Jesus takes the traditions and what we call the Law (God's instructions), and explains their true intent, which is to allow our hearts to be changed. This ultimately affects our actions. Heart change should be first; then, a change in actions will follow.

In Matthew 5, verses 27 and 28 Jesus says:

²⁷"You have heard the commandment that says, 'You must not commit adultery.' ²⁸ But I say, anyone who even looks at a woman with lust has already committed adultery with her in his heart."

Again, we have Jesus quoting a commandment from God, or you could say that we have Jesus quoting an instruction (a law) from God. The instruction says don't commit adultery. Jesus then follows up by saying "remember, I'm the only One that knows the true intent of that instruction, and I'm going to take the discussion a little deeper." The Law says don't commit adultery (physical action), but I say anyone who looks at a woman with lust has already committed adultery with her in his HEART (heart action/thought). If we are to be honest with ourselves, men and women may often lust over someone else in their minds (in their heart), but we hide these thoughts. Maybe that thought never makes it out into an action. Praise God that it doesn't; however, Jesus is saying – the thought is just as bad as the action. Now, this is not a license to go commit the act! Jesus is telling us that it's the thought that CAN turn into the action, so I need you to work on not having that thought at all!

Now, let's define lust, because I think we can sometimes limit lust to sexual lust. Lust, however, goes beyond that. Lust can be sexual or physical, but it can be more than that. Let's look at the definition of lust. Lust means to have a desire for, to long for, to seek something you don't have. So, I may have lust for a person sexually, and we know that's wrong. But, I may also have lust for material things, like a car or a better job. I may lust for food. Lust, at the core, is wanting something better than what I have.

Lust OFTEN manifests (shows up) in a sexual way. A man may look at a woman and begin to fantasize about a sexual relationship with that person; or a woman may look at a man and do the same. Now, let's go deeper. What about when a woman looks at a man that is treating his wife really well and thinks "I wish my husband treated me like that..."? You guessed it! That is also lust.

I think we have to be careful that we don't get fooled into thinking that lust is only sexual. Lust is desiring something you don't have. So, Jesus is saying – If a man looks at a woman and desires to have her for whatever reason, that is lust. It could be sexual, it could be because it's perceived she'll treat him better than his own wife does, or it could be because she's a great cook. Same with a woman. She may lust after a man – desire what she doesn't have – because he's polite, because he's a gentleman, or because of the house he lives in. I'm trying to use some random examples to get the point across. We need to be careful here. I may not look at a woman with sexual desires, but I may desire other things about that person. Jesus is saying – DON'T desire what you don't have.

I haven't even mentioned money or position or power. How many people desire someone because of those things?

By the way, this is so serious, that Jesus follows up with these instruction in verses 29 and 30:

"²⁹ So if your eye—even your good eye— causes you to lust, gouge it out and throw it away. It is better for you to lose one part of your body than for your whole body to be thrown into hell. ³⁰ And if your hand—even your stronger hand—causes you to sin, cut it off and throw it away. It is better for you to lose one part of your body than for your whole body to be thrown into hell."

I think that Jesus is trying to make a big point. If you desire more than you have when it comes to your spouse, this is so serious of a problem that you'd be better to gouge out YOUR EYE so that you don't lust after that person. Cut off your hand so that you don't want to touch that person! This is serious because He mentions "hell" at the end of that verse.

As Christians, we often say a sin is a sin. There are no greater sins than others. However, in the bible over and over, hell is mentioned very often with sexual sin. I'm not here to get into a theological debate at this point about sexual sin being worse that some other sin, I'm simply pointing out that apparently the heart behind pursuing sexual sin is something that Jesus really wants us to clean up! It has consequences, and those consequences can include hell. YOUCH! This is a "pay attention" moment!

Lust from the beginning...

I want to back up quite a bit in the bible, to further explain this point. Let's look at Adam and Eve in the garden of Eden. When satan tempts Eve, he offers her more than she has. She has PARADISE. There's no evil, other than the serpent himself. Even though the serpent (satan) is evil, he can not physically harm Eve. However, he can tempt her. This just went from a physical action to the heart action (or thoughts). He can't hurt her physically, but he can tempt her heart, her mind – which ultimately results in a physical action that changes the course of history for all of us.

So, life is perfect. No sin....no pain....no death.....no hunger...no thirst....no tears.... She has everything that she needs as a human. God has provided. However, God still allows her and Adam "free will".

There are two significant fruit trees in the garden. One is the Tree of Life. One is the Tree of the Knowledge of Good and Evil. At this point, they have ONE instruction from God. The Law of Moses has 613 instructions from God, just to put this in perspective. They have one instruction – don't eat from that Tree of the Knowledge of Good and Evil. At this point, Adam and Eve only know GOOD. Eating from this tree allows them to know GOOD AND EVIL.

When satan appears, he appeals to Eve with the ONE thing she doesn't have – more knowledge. He tempts her with the desire to know more. satan says "Did God really say that you must not eat the fruit from any of the trees in the garden?" Eve responds "Of course we may eat the fruit from the trees in the garden – except for that one tree. In fact, we can't even touch it, or we will die". satan says "You won't die!" This is a lie from satan.... Then he says "God knows that your eyes will be opened as soon as you eat it, and you will be LIKE GOD, knowing both good and evil".

Ok, evil is a bad thing, right? We know that, right? But, did Eve know that? NO. What satan did was tempt her with the one thing that she didn't know. He created a desire in her to know more – more than she had access to. Creating that curiosity for her created a lust in her. I want to know more. I deserve to know more. satan could not attack her physically, but he tempted her heart, her mind. Then, her desire to have what she didn't have – or her desire to have what she COULDN'T have – led to her physical action of not only touching the fruit, but eating it as well. Boom....sin entered the world!

Same lust today...

As I council couples today, one of their biggest problems is that same temptation 5,780+ years later – the temptation that we deserve more. It's the ultimate generational curse! satan's goal is to tempt you, in your mind....in your heart....that you deserve more from a spouse. Maybe the temptation is that you deserve more sex or better sex. Maybe that temptation is that you deserve better treatment. Maybe that temptation is that you deserve more attention. I could go on and on. satan's goal is to make you think that you deserve more – that creates lust – if you don't clean the lust out of your heart – that lust can lead to a physical act. It seems like a good thing in the moment, just like it did for Eve. Then, it creates a lifetime of chaos and consequences that you regret the rest of your life, just like it did for Eve. It always affects others, like your immediate family, possibly for generations to come. Eve's failure is still affecting us today!

I believe that satan knew that if he could get Eve to desire something she couldn't have (which is lust), he knew he would have a tool to use for generations to come.

Now, at this point, you might ask....how does lust for money create adultery? It's pretty clear that sexual lust can create physical adultery, right? When we lust for money, and it becomes an idol to us, we begin to put many things before God. We begin to "worship" worldly things, and we begin to put those things before God. So, now, the adultery is effectively "cheating on God".

We need to be clear here about the damage that lust can cause for our relationship with our spouse and for our relationship with God. I struggled with lust for many years. I lusted for sexual pleasures. I lusted for a calmer mind. I lusted for physical or material things like houses, cars, boats, motorcycles, etc. I worked hard, and thought I deserved more than I had in every area. That lust, which I allowed to grow in my heart, led to physical actions. I pursued pornography or worse to satisfy the sexual pleasures. I became great "friends" with Jack Daniels to satisfy my mind racing issues. I bought bigger houses, and more expensive cars, and bigger boats, and expensive watches, and louder Harley Davidson motorcycles. Each of these things pushed me further and further away from God. Each of these things created lasting consequences. While I'm thankful now to have a testimony to share about how Jesus healed me, saved me, and redeemed me, I have a lot to be ashamed about in my past. I share it openly to try and help people, but that doesn't mean that I'm proud of it. I still have consequences today with broken relationships, and I still have to fight off mental thoughts of shame and guilt. But, ultimately, I had to learn that ALL of these things that led to my sins fit into one category – LUST. I constantly wanted more than I had, I constantly thought I deserved more than I had, and I allowed that lust to manifest into sin and adultery. I put so many things before God. I was cheating on Him, so to speak. He redeemed me through Blood of the Lamb, and that's why I want to spend the rest of my life helping others understand why Jesus would say words like these! He knows the destruction that comes with lust. He knows the lasting effects. He knows the guilt and shame. He knows that if you learn to fight off the lust in your heart – you will not allow that lust to turn into reality.

Bounce your heart…

One last thing on this topic. In my journey to deal with sexual lust and pornography issues, I participated in a men's bible study that was specifically designed to help men. I won't name the book or the study, out of respect, but it was a "bible based" curriculum that gave TERRIBLE advice.

Let me give you a scenario that men may struggle with. Maybe women as well. I'm going to try and not give you too many visuals. I just want to make a point. Let's say I'm driving down the road and I see a beautiful woman walking down the sidewalk. Simply staring at that woman can create lust in my mind. It can create fantasies in my mind. It could lead me to do something stupid to pursue her, or maybe fester in my mind until I would go look at pornography.

So, I read this book and it has a key phrase for men – "Bounce Your Eyes". So, the idea is that when I see her (as I laid out in the scenario above), I have the self-discipline to "bounce my eyes" away from her. Here's the problem. That's training a physical action to override a physical action. Bounce your eyes instead of staring at her. The problem wasn't my eyes. It was my heart. While the "bounce your eyes" theory sounds good, it doesn't deal with the root of the issue. I needed to learn to "Bounce My Heart"!

Jesus doesn't say "Change your physical situation." He says "Change your heart!" He doesn't say "Bounce your eyes". He says "Bounce your heart"! As you do this, you know what happens? You get to know Jesus better, and He gets to know you better!

Divorce...

Divorce is an epidemic today in America. Statistically, well over half of the marriages in America end in divorce. When you look at first marriages, half of them end in divorce, statistically. When you look at 2nd and 3rd marriages, well over half end in divorce. Unfortunately, these #'s hold true among those in ministry as well, which is shocking!

We seem to have gotten to a point in our society where many have a mentality to just try out marriage and see how it works. If it satisfies us, great. If it becomes less satisfying or too hard, we'll just take the easy way out with a divorce.

What may surprise you is that divorce was a big enough problem in Jesus's time, that He addressed it here in scripture. Now, we don't know what the divorce rates were back then, and we don't need to know that data. We just need to know what Jesus expects of us.

In Matthew 5, verses 31 and 32, Jesus says:

[31] "You have heard the law that says, 'A man can divorce his wife by merely giving her a written notice of divorce.' [32] But I say that a man who divorces his wife, unless she has been unfaithful, causes her to commit adultery. And anyone who marries a divorced woman also commits adultery."

I'm not trying to sound too sarcastic here, but I thought the "Law" was just simply too hard for us to follow as believers in Jesus???? Yet, once again, Jesus takes the Law, better explains it, and makes it harder for us.

Maybe, you are surprised to hear that the Law (God's instructions) allowed for a divorce to happen. In Deuteronomy 24, Moses gives instructions on what to do with a divorce. You can go there and read that chapter to get more information, but Moses says "Suppose a man marries a woman but she does not please him. Having discovered something wrong with her, he writes a document of divorce, hands it to her, and sends her away from his house."

What we see here is that divorce was extremely easy to do back then under the Law. As much as we hear about the Law being too hard to follow, this is a shocker, right? She doesn't please the man… he simply writes her a letter to divorce. It's a good thing that the courts don't make it that easy for us today!!

Now, let's look just a little deeper into their culture. Today, we look at success from the standpoint of bank accounts or other material things (cars, properties, etc.). In other words, success is about money for us, or it's about power from position. Back in the time that Moses wrote this, money and power were available to some, but success was also measured in the amount of livestock you owned and the number of children you had. So, if a woman was not capable of becoming pregnant and producing offspring, a man would not be "pleased" with her. A man would see something "wrong" with her. Most often, divorces happened because she couldn't produce offspring.

Honestly, it blows my mind that it was easy and acceptable back then. Now, Jesus comes along and says I understand completely what marriage is supposed to be. I am going to "preach it up" a little. We know from other scriptures, like Ephesians 5, that marriage between a man and a woman represents Jesus and His Church. That's us! God designed marriage to represent Jesus and His Church. Jesus died for His Church! He didn't divorce it when it didn't act right…. He didn't divorce it when He wasn't pleased with it….He didn't divorce it when He found something wrong with it. He died for it when He found everything wrong with it!! Jesus, as the groom, will never give up on us as the bride!

So, Jesus says, I know the Law, the instructions, say you can divorce, but I need you to understand that God doesn't want that. In Mark 10, we get more detail on this that helps us better understand Jesus's intent here. In Mark 10, verses 2 through 9, it says:

² Some Pharisees came and tried to trap him with this question: "Should a man be allowed to divorce his wife?" ³ Jesus answered them with a question: "What did Moses say in the law about divorce?" ⁴ "Well, he permitted it," they replied. "He said a man can give his wife a written notice of divorce and send her away."

⁵ But Jesus responded, "He wrote this commandment only as a concession to your hard hearts. ⁶ But 'God made them male and female' from the beginning of creation. ⁷ 'This explains why a man leaves his father and mother and is joined to his wife, ⁸ and the two are united into one.' Since they are no longer two but one, ⁹ let no one split apart what God has joined together."

Did you see what Jesus says there? "He wrote this commandment only as a concession to your hard hearts." Then, He ends with "Let no one split apart what God has joined together".

This entire discussion has been about understanding the Heart of the Father, and allowing Him to change our hearts – not our actions. Jesus makes it clear here that God allowed the action due to a hard heart. But, when we allow our hearts to more align with the Heart of God, the Heart of Jesus, we'll know that He doesn't intend for anyone to get a divorce – let NO ONE split apart what God has joined together.

So, once again, this is a heart issue. If we are selfish, we just run when things get tough, or we run when we don't get what we want or expect out of the marriage. But, Jesus's message is about giving up selfishness. The more each of you pursue heart change and pursue giving up selfishness, the more you grow closer together. You begin to focus on each other – not on what you need to be pleased.

The big 3 things that ruin a marriage...

Let's go back to Adam and Eve. In that story, I clearly see three things that happen, and all three are still causing problems today:

1. satan tempts them with what they don't have.
2. Adam is passive and allows Eve to fail.
3. They blame shift instead of taking responsibility.

When I counsel couples, I can generally put all of their issues into one or more of these three categories. As we already discussed, satan works hard to make each of us think we deserve more. A lot of failures in marriages, especially when an affair happens, tie back to one or both thinking they deserve more. Then, they see something in someone else, or at least THINK they see something in someone else that looks like it'll fulfill that missing piece. This is lust at the core, or maybe we'd say – the "grass looks greener on that side of the fence".

Next, we have the passive male. In Genesis 3, it says, "She took some of the fruit and ate it. Then, she turned to her husband, who was with her, and he ate it too." Eve didn't have to go searching for Adam. He was right there, watching her fail to the one instruction they had. And...HE DID NOTHING! He allowed her to do it. Then, he followed her lead and ate it too. The passive male....still haunts us today. The man doesn't accept his responsibility in the home, and now expects the mom, his wife, to do all the teaching to the children....all the spiritualizing and teaching of scripture....all the hard work in making the family desire to have some Jesus in it. We, as men, have this built-in desire to go to work, come home, and "veg out" to relax. And, we become lazy and passive husbands and fathers. That's exactly what satan wants us to do. We are supposed to be the spiritual leaders, but we become the passive Adam. Then, we wonder why a wife would "lust" after a better man.

Finally, we blame. Adam blamed Eve, and he blamed God. "It was the woman you gave me". He took no responsibility for his actions. He blamed. If you learn nothing more in this book, please learn that blaming God never turns out good! Yet, many of us do it...

Do you see how this disrupts marriages today? We think we deserve more....we have the passive male....and when things go wrong, we blame each other AND God. It all started in the garden, and it's led to an excepted divorce rate between 50% and 70%, depending on how you look at the numbers (first marriages vs 2nd/3rd marriages).

Jesus is saying, "Protect your heart against these lies from satan!" "Don't take the easy way out." If you allow Jesus to change your heart, and your spouse allows Jesus to change their heart, NO MAN WILL SPLIT APART WHAT GOD HAS BROUGHT TOGETHER!

Fight for your marriage! Make the changes in your selfish nature that you need to make to have a better marriage! Fight off the lust of seeing "greener grass" somewhere else! Don't be passive and allow sin to happen! Don't blame – Take full responsibility for your actions!!! All these things allow Jesus to know you more!!

Questions and Application for Chapter 8
1. Do you desire things that you don't have?
2. Which is a struggle for you? Lust for someone? Lust for material things? Lust for food? All the above?
3. Now that satan's "game" has been exposed, will you fight it?
4. Do you realize that your actions affect others?
5. Which of the "big 3" affects your marriage or relationships the most? (This chapter is focused on marriages, but I believe these things can affect all relationships and friendships. For example, a child could want a parent that is more lenient like their friend's parent...).
6. Challenge – Begin to recognize the desire to want what you can't have. Our society may say "you are just dreaming for better things." However, you now know that it becomes a dangerous thing, called lust, that can ruin your life and relationships. As you identify lust in your life, ask God to take it away!

Prayer
"Father, thank you for exposing what lust is and how dangerous it is in our lives! Please help me to identify the areas where I struggle with lust so that I can allow You to change my thoughts and desires. Father, please help couples to recognize the simple things that satan uses to try and destroy marriages every day, and please help us to fight to save our marriages and fight to help others save their marriages. Father, thank you for exposing satan's game. Help us to expose it to others as we help build each other up. Help me to be satisfied with all the wonderful things that You have already given me!"

9

how we treat people matters...

Promises...
As we proceed into the Sermon on the Mount, we are seeing a theme develop. How we treat people shows where our hearts are. In Matthew 5, verses 33-36, Jesus discusses vows, or maybe we would say the word "promises". He says:

> [33] "You have also heard that our ancestors were told, 'You must not break your vows; you must carry out the vows you make to the LORD.' [34] But I say, do not make any vows! Do not say, 'By heaven!' because heaven is God's throne. [35] And do not say, 'By the earth!' because the earth is his footstool. And do not say, 'By Jerusalem!' for Jerusalem is the city of the great King. [36] Do not even say, 'By my head!' for you can't turn one hair white or black. [37] Just say a simple, 'Yes, I will,' or 'No, I won't.' Anything beyond this is from the evil one."

You might be familiar with the phrase "Let your yes's be yes's and your no's be no's". Let's be honest with where we are in our society. We live in world where a person's words mean almost nothing. This is an unfortunate reality for much of the world.

Remember, I'm differentiating the "world" from the "church". In the world, people say yes when they know they mean no. People say yes or no in an emotional moment, without truly thinking through what they are saying. People will change their mind and not honor their promises of yes and no, depending on how the circumstance benefits them in that moment.

Most of our parents or grandparents lived in a society in American where the world was run on a handshake and on your word. If two people agreed on something and shook hands, it was written in stone! Today, on the other hand, we can agree on something…sign a contract….have a witness that notarizes the contract….and then sue to get out of the contract for no reason other than we are tired of that agreement, or we have changed our minds, or we have found a better deal. It's very common now to promise and then change, from the smallest and simplest of promises, up to the most thorough and complex of promises.

Now, let's look at this through the lens of Jesus – from a heart perspective. When you make a promise and break it, you are letting someone down. You are breaking trust. You lose integrity. Jesus basically says "Stick with your commitments, or simply say NO." Sometimes, it's hard to commit to a definite Yes. But, sometimes, we want to say No, but that seems harsh…so we say yes…knowing we'll back out in a soft way at some point later. Over time, people learn to not trust us. Over time, this hurts people. Over time, we get more passive in not being able to fulfill our commitments.

This should be simple and easy. Stop and think before you answer. If you say yes, do it. If you say no, don't do it. Don't overcomplicate this!

Then, Jesus gives specific examples….don't swear by heaven…. or by earth….or by Jerusalem….or by your head. To understand this, we need to look at the customs of their culture. Remember, the Jewish religious leaders often created what I call "a fence within a fence". If they didn't understand an instruction (a law), they would create a more strict tradition, just to make sure they didn't come close to breaking an instruction. I would argue that this was done with a pure heart, trying hard to please God. "We want to make so sure that we don't violate any instructions of God – so, we'll make them all harder – we'll fence ourselves in tighter – just to make sure we don't break that commandment."

This leads to traditions and rules and man-made "religion". (Side note – these traditions are what we most often object to when it comes to the Law of Moses.... It's not the Law itself. It's the tradition or rule that was NEVER supposed to be there!).

When it came to vows, the Jewish leaders severely overcomplicated it. They invented a system to determine if a vow had to be kept. It was not considered to be a sin to break a vow, unless that vow was made explicitly in the name of God. Maybe, that's where we get the term "I swear to God".... If somebody made a promise or a vow in the name of heaven, it was not binding. If somebody made a promise or a vow in the name of the gold in the temple, it was not binding. If someone made a promise or took a vow in God's name, they had to do it. If the vow or promise was taken in the name of heaven, or in the name of the earth, or in the name of Jerusalem, or in the name of your own head, there was a way out of the promise. It was either a "No"...or at best, a "Maybe".

People began to make their vows and oaths and promises in the name of things other than God to give them a way out in case they didn't want to keep their word, or in case they changed their mind. This reminds me of something that we used to do as kids. If someone asked me a question, I would lie to them, while crossing my fingers. I had my fingers crossed! Gotcha! I didn't "lie"...I didn't break a "vow"...I had my fingers crossed! That's essentially what the people were doing. They had their own system of "crossing their fingers" when they made vows! Now, Jesus is trying to get this back to something simple. Say yes if you plan to keep the vow/promise. Say no if you aren't going to keep the vow/promise. Tradition is complicated. Jesus is simple!!!!

This is part of what's wrong with the church today. We read scripture, and then complicate the simple commands of God by creating traditions. If we can strip that away and get back to the simplicity of doing what God says, it's just easier all the way around!

So....of course, the enemy shows up, convinces us to complicate things, and then those traditions cause problems. Then, as our society progresses, it gets even more complicated. Back then, if I made a vow in the name of the temple, you knew I was at best 50/50 on completing that vow. Today, we say yes when we know in that moment that we are telling a big fat lie. We have no intention sometimes of doing what we say we will do. Sadly, I can bring the church back into this conversation when I say this. Jesus is saying be honest. Do what you say you will do. Stop and think before you make a promise you can't keep. This often involves giving up your selfishness of what is making you want to change your answer from Yes to No.

This applies to so many aspects of our lives. We will often say "Yes" to a request. In that moment, we mean "Yes" – until it becomes inconvenient. Then, we change it to "No". We just talked about divorce in the previous chapter. That would apply here as well. We say Yes to marriage, until it becomes more convenient to say No. Then, we divorce.

We can look at this from an integrity standpoint, from a commitment standpoint, from a courage standpoint, and from a complication versus simplicity standpoint. I want to be clear. This is not saying there is no room for changing your mind. There are times when you need to make changes. There are times when circumstances change. This is about your heart. Remember, Jesus is calling them out for making all these things that they could make a vow to – when they know they just need to say NO. Want to be known by Jesus?? Just read the simple instructions, and do it! Don't plan a way out with your words. If you say Yes, stick with it. If you need to say No, just say No! Let me add another option. You can say "I don't know yet". However, don't say "I don't know" when you know you'll say "No"!!! Nobody does that, right? Let your Yes be Yes. Let your No be No.

Revenge...

What is one of the most natural emotions or feelings that we can have when we've been wronged or hurt? REVENGE! "I'll get you back for what you did to me!" It just comes natural, right? As soon as we are wronged, we want to return the favor back to them. This can be something innocent. Maybe, you pulled a prank on me. Now, I want to get revenge....and pull a prank on you. This can also be very damaging and dangerous. Maybe you talked about me behind my back, so I want to get you back. Maybe you stole from me, so I want to steal from you. Maybe, you sucker punched me, so I want to sucker punch you back. I could go on and on, but I think you get the point. Revenge comes natural.

Jesus says, "Even the Law permits revenge, right?" In Matthew 5, verses 38-42, Jesus addresses something that is hard for each of us. He says:

> 38 "You have heard the law that says the punishment must match the injury: 'An eye for an eye, and a tooth for a tooth.' 39 But I say, do not resist an evil person! If someone slaps you on the right cheek, offer the other cheek also. 40 If you are sued in court and your shirt is taken from you, give your coat, too. 41 If a soldier demands that you carry his gear for a mile, carry it two miles. 42 Give to those who ask, and don't turn away from those who want to borrow."

It was their custom to punish a crime with the same crime. An eye for an eye...a tooth for a tooth. The Law is very clear about this. If a man murders another man, then that man would also be killed. The punishment was permitted, or instructed, to fit the crime. Not only is it natural to seek revenge, but the instructions of God permitted it!

Then, Jesus comes along, and once again says --- "But I want to change your heart." Yes, the instructions of God permit it, but God is a merciful God, and He intends for you to be merciful as well. Remember, we are made in God's image. God seeks those who have hearts that line up with His. He is merciful, only going to judgment and punishment when the mercy is not accepted....due to lack of change (repentance).

When we seek revenge, it makes it harder to forgive. We haven't gotten to forgiveness yet, but we will soon. When we seek revenge, it creates bitterness, and bitterness eats away at us to the point of destruction at times. Jesus is setting up some big things that He's about to teach us. We break these chapters in Matthew 5, 6, and 7 up into smaller chunks by their themes, but Jesus was not giving a segmented sermon. Each point was meant to build for the next point. Jesus was saying – "For me to talk about forgiveness, I'll have to adjust your thoughts on a few things. First, let's change how you look at revenge." This about having to actively assess a situation to go against the norm of our human nature as well as to go against the norm of society.

Love your enemies...

This leads to His next point. He says in verses 43 through 48:

> 43 "You have heard the law that says, 'Love your neighbor' and hate your enemy. 44 But I say, love your enemies! Pray for those who persecute you! 45 In that way, you will be acting as true children of your Father in heaven. For he gives his sunlight to both the evil and the good, and he sends rain on the just and the unjust alike. 46 If you love only those who love you, what reward is there for that? Even corrupt tax collectors do that much. 47 If you are kind only to your friends, how are you different from anyone else? Even pagans do that. 48 But you are to be perfect, even as your Father in heaven is perfect."

Ok....it's hard enough to not seek revenge.....NOW YOU WANT ME TO LOVE MY ENEMIES???

Jesus says – YES!!

Once again....Jesus is making the instructions harder! The instructions, the Law, says Love your neighbor and hate your enemy. That's really not that hard, right? Love those who are good to you. Love those who are your friends. That's easy. Now, hate those that are bad to you. Hate those that come against you. That's easy. Those instructions from God are relatively easy!

Jesus says, I'm gonna make this harder for you. Yes, love your neighbors, AND love your enemies. Pray for those that hurt you. It's not that Jesus is trying to make it harder, it's that He's trying to get you closer to the heart of the Father. Maybe you are starting to pick up on the theme that having the heart of the Father, or allowing Jesus and His instructions to mold your heart to that of the Father, is a huge piece for being known by Jesus!

The Father loves those who are good, and He loves those who are evil. He doesn't reward those who are evil. Those who are evil don't inherit the Kingdom. Those who are evil will face His wrath. However, or nonetheless, He loves them. If you want to have the heart of the Father, you can't just love those that are easy to love. You have to love those that are hard to love. Tax collectors and pagans can love those that are good to them. Remember, tax collectors were despised. Obviously, pagans aren't good people because they worship other gods.

Jesus is saying a worldly heart can love those who are friends.... those who are good to you....those who treat you well. But, to have a GODLY heart, the heart of the Father, we have to love the unlovable. Don't seek revenge from those that hurt you. Pray for them. Love them. You want to be set apart for God? Remember, that's the definition of Holy – to be set apart. You want to be Holy, set apart for God? Treat those that hurt you the same way you'd treat those that do good for you.

WOW! That's a game changer for these people that Jesus is talking to, and it's a game changer for us! God sends the rain for the good and the evil at the same time. He gives the sunlight to the good and the evil at the same time. He gives His love to the good and the evil at the same time. He does not reward the evil, nor is Jesus asking us to reward the evil. He asked us to love them, to pray for them, to not seek to hurt them back. He never says reward them. I just want to make sure we keep this discussion and point in balance. He doesn't say let them continue to hurt you. You can get away from them, you can set boundaries for them to not be around you, and you can obviously not reward them. Those are ok. Now, at the same time, you can love them (patience, kindness, not rude, etc – from 1 Corinthians 13), and you can pray for them.

This is sort of hard to live out…

When I first left my career and went into ministry, I thought life was about to be easy, right? Ministry is going to be fun and rewarding, right? Wow, was I wrong! It is fun. It is rewarding. It does put a bigger target on your back from satan.

I went to work for a church, and was asked immediately to do things that go against scripture. Here's the thing – I didn't leave a "$1 million +" per year salary and my sinful life behind to simply play church or to play "church job". I left my career to do what Jesus said, and to teach others.

When unbiblical things happened, I lovingly, with prayer and scripture, confronted the pastor. I was literally crying as I talked to him about how much I loved him, and as I told him how much he meant to me. His teachings had literally been used by God to draw me out of my sinful path to hell. When he disagreed with me, I simply resigned. We hugged. We both cried. I left.

Within days, the narrative changed. All of a sudden, I was the bad guy. I went back into his office for another meeting. My wife had warned me this was a bad idea. God had shown her. I went anyway, thinking I was doing the right thing. In that meeting, I was accused of things I didn't do, and he was turning things back around on me. I failed….I lost my temper…and I cussed him. It was a mistake, I realized it immediately, and I asked for his forgiveness.

I left, only to realize this new reality of how I would be labeled the bad guy that cussed out the pastor. I was devastated. I was trying to follow Jesus with ALL my heart. I was trying to lovingly correct him. I did make a mistake in that second meeting, and I'll own that. But, what had happened? From "tears and I love you's" to "I'm the bad guy". I questioned if I was supposed to be in ministry. I questioned if I was right about my decision to change careers. I questioned my own salvation. I questioned everything.

I kept reading God's word. I had never read through the entire bible before, so that was a journey I had been on and wanted to continue. I didn't give up, and I read more. Within days, I came to this scripture – 1 Peter 3 verses 8-10:

"⁸ Finally, all of you should be of one mind. Sympathize with each other. Love each other as brothers and sisters. Be tenderhearted, and keep a humble attitude. ⁹ Don't repay evil for evil. Don't retaliate with insults when people insult you. Instead, pay them back with a blessing. That is what God has called you to do, and he will grant you his blessing."

Don't repay evil with evil? I'm ready to walk into that church and punch the pastor in the mouth while he's preaching! I wanted revenge. Do you see where I'm going?

I hate to admit this, but I even called the head of security and asked him what they would do to me if I came in during a sermon, got on stage, and punched the pastor in front of everyone. He told me he'd let me get one punch in before I was tackled and arrested for assault. Did you hear that? The head of security even knew I was the one in the right!

But…..Peter says DON'T REPAY EVIL WITH EVIL. Don't retaliate with insults when you've been insulted. Instead, pay them back with a blessing. This is what God would want, and He will give you a blessing!

Don't those words sound just like Jesus's words in Matthew? Don't seek revenge. Pray for them. Love them. It'll gain you the heart of the Father!

For the next 6 months, every time I drove by that church, which was often, I prayed for God to bless them. That's what Peter said to do. "Pay them back with a blessing". So, I prayed for them to have a blessing from God. Was it hard? You better believe it was hard. Honestly, it still drives a little knife in my back even to tell this story. I can feel myself tense up a little as I write. What does that mean? I'm still working on forgiveness, almost 10 years later. I'm still working on the pain. I'm still working on praying for them.

I don't have the heart of the Father yet, but I'm trying to obey His word and get there.

I literally switched from anger to tears as I'm writing this. I'm serious. Jesus doesn't expect us to get to the heart of the Father in one prayer or in one day, but He expects us to know the expectations and to try. I'm trying. It's easier now than it was 5 years ago. I actually feel sorry for them now. But, I want to be honest – there are days I'd still like to punch him. What does that mean? I need to read 1 Peter 3 again….I need to read Matthew 5 again…and I need pray for my enemy and be loving to them. I need to keep blessing them. What's my reward? My reward is more of the Father's heart. My reward is the peace and joy that comes with forgiveness. My reward is letting that bitterness go.

As I learn more and more about the Father, I realize how bad He hurts when we do the same to Him. That's part of what hurts so bad about this situation for me. I want to contrast another scenario that happened to me.

In 2022, I was attacked by a man because I tried to tell him about Jesus. He was trespassing at my house, on our farm, and he attacked me for no reason, as he was in a place he shouldn't have been. The difference between him and the pastor mentioned above is that he didn't know Jesus. I expect him to want to hurt me more than I would expect to be hurt by the pastor.

Forgiving him was almost instantaneous. I hurt for him. I long for him to know Jesus. As he attacked me, and I had to defend myself, I prayed for him out loud to his face as we waited for the helicopter to take him to the hospital. It makes no sense, but he was easy to love when he was my enemy. I want him to know Jesus!

However, the first scenario is about a man that is supposed to teach me scripture, not be a hypocrite. He's supposed to help me heal, not be the enemy that hurt me.

Do you see where I'm going? Sometimes, it hurts worse when the enemy is "in the church". It hurts worse when the enemy is your shepherd. It hurts worse when your enemy knows better.

Both are or were my "enemies". I pray for them both now, because Jesus said to. I don't seek revenge on either. I'm trying to love them. It's hard. Jesus never said it was easy, but He did say it makes you more known by Him!

I shared these stories in the hope that it helps you live out these scriptures. I shared these stories in the hope that it helps you understand that we need to keep doing it, even if it still hurts years later. I shared these stories in the hope that it helps you and me be better known by Jesus!!!

Questions and Application for Chapter 9
1. Do you say "yes" when you know it's a "no"? Do you say "yes" when it's really a "I don't know"?
2. What makes you say Yes in that moment? Is it fear? Is it lack of self-control to stop and think? Is it a fear that you will be rejected if you say No?
3. Do thoughts of revenge come natural to you?
4. Do you have an "enemy" that you need to love and bless?
5. Have you been hurt by someone in the church? Does that affect your desire to go to church because of that hurt? Has that affected your relationship with God? Have you blamed God?
6. Challenge – Think of one or more person(s) that you consider an enemy. Pray a prayer for them to be blessed by God.

Prayer
"Father, first of all, thank you for loving me and blessing me when I was your enemy. Thank you for loving me and blessing me when I continue to be your enemy. Sometimes, I'm your enemy without realizing it in the moment. Thank you for not seeking revenge on me when I deserved it. Help me to show that same mercy and love to my enemies. Help me to know how to set a boundary with them, while loving them and blessing them. Please give me more of Your heart Father. Father, I'm sorry if I've allowed a person in the church affect how I look at church or how I look at You. Please forgive me for that!"

10

are you just trying to look good for others to see???

Good deeds again...
As we move into Matthew chapter 6, Jesus begins to shift His discussion a bit. It's still about the heart, but the shift is about what is driving your actions. Are you doing the good thing that you are doing because it's the right thing to do, or are you doing the good thing because you want people to see that good thing that you are doing?

He starts off in verse 1 talking about good deeds. Jesus says:

"Watch out! Don't do your good deeds publicly, to be admired by others, for you will lose the reward from your Father in heaven."

We've already talked in detail about good deeds in Chapter 5. By the time we get to this point in the discussion, the assumption is that we understand that good deeds are a must for us as believers in Jesus. Now, we are focusing on the motive behind doing the good deed. Jesus starts out with an emphatic – "Watch out"! In other words, "Pay attention!" He says "Don't do your good deeds in public, to be admired by others." Let's pause right here and make sure this doesn't look like a contrast to what Jesus said back when we were discussing salt and light. In Matthew 5, Jesus says "Let your good deeds shine out for all to see, so that EVERYONE WILL PRAISE YOUR HEAVENLY FATHER." Then, in Matthew 6, He says "Don't do your good deeds publicly, to be admired by others".

We are supposed to do good deeds. We are supposed to do good deeds in public for all to see. The difference is our motive. Or, you could say, "where's your heart?" Option A is that you do it to bring praise to the Father. Option B is that you do it to bring praise to yourself. Option A is good. Option B is not good. Bringing praise to the Father is good. Bringing praise to yourself LIMITS your reward. He clearly states, if you do it to be admired by others or to bring praise to yourself, you will lose the reward from your Father in heaven.

Two important things here. First of all, we should do good deeds because it's a command from Jesus, but we also learn that we get rewards for those good deeds. Good deeds not only prove our faith in Jesus, but gain us rewards! Second, make sure the Father is getting praised for the good deed, not you.

Let's give an example of when we do a good deed for someone. We do a good dead, and we are immediately thanked. That feels good in that moment to be appreciated. That's a reward in that moment. Then, maybe at church or another public gathering, that person will tell others about the good deed that happened. So, we have a choice to make at that point. Accept the praise of others and enjoy that very momentary reward; or, we can redirect that praise to the Father, so that we get eternal rewards. Jesus is clear – Do the good deed. Give praise to the Father. Get the eternal reward!

We live in a society that is overwhelmed with social media influence right now. I wonder what Jesus would think if He read some of the social media accounts of churches and Christians that post their good deeds out for the world to see, bringing the attention to themselves. We live in a "me first" society. Jesus makes it clear that

Christ followers need to live with a "Father first" mentality. It will be the opposite of what the world does. It may be the opposite of what some churches do. Give praise to the Father for the good deed, and you get the eternal reward. If they take the praise for themselves on social media, they will get a reward only in that moment, and it will only be praised by men. I don't know about you, but I'll pass up all praise from people for 1 praise from the Father!!

Giving to those in need...

Jesus then transitions to giving to the needy. It's a different action, but the same lesson or message from Jesus:

> "² When you give to someone in need, don't do as the hypocrites do—blowing trumpets in the synagogues and streets to call attention to their acts of charity! I tell you the truth, they have received all the reward they will ever get. ³ But when you give to someone in need, don't let your left hand know what your right hand is doing. ⁴ Give your gifts in private, and your Father, who sees everything, will reward you."

Similar to good deeds, we will start with the assumption that you are giving to someone in need. Maybe, we could expand this discussion to include giving to ministries, who then in turn give to those in need. Are you giving for the right reason? Are you giving so that you can brag to everyone about how much you gave? Are you giving because it's an instruction from God, and you receive rewards for it?

These are questions that you have to wrestle with. It's between you and God. First off, if you aren't giving, forget the rest of the discussion. You're simply not going to get any rewards. Next, if you are giving, or if you begin to give, now, what is your motive? Is it to be obedient? Is to draw praise to yourself?

It's your choice just like good deeds. First, do it. Next, do it for the right reason. You can let everyone know, and they will praise you. You will look good in front of them. Or, give and don't tell anyone. Now, it's between you and God only, and He rewards you.

With good deeds, it was do it in public – Give praise to the Father – Get rewarded! With giving, it is do it privately – Don't tell anyone – Get rewarded!

Giving for the wrong reason...

Back when I was in sales, and I was making a lot of money, I gave, but I gave for the wrong reason. For me, it was the only Godly thing I was doing, so I look back on it and realize I was probably trying to "pay off" my sins by writing big checks to the church. I never thought that in the moment, but I can see that as I look back and evaluate my life.

I didn't necessarily stand and brag about it from the streets, but I sure enjoyed it when people brought it up. I would try to act humble about it, but the truth is that I was displaying false humility as I soaked up the reward and praise I was getting right then. My hope is that I gave in a way at times to get an eternal reward, but there is a reality that I've already received many of the rewards for that giving – because my heart was in the wrong place. I'm trying to give you as many personal examples as I can so that you can see how much Jesus can change a person who is committed to learning and living out these scriptures. It's a testimony at this point. I can't change the bad things I've done, but I can give the Father credit for redeeming and restoring me through a renewed and passionate relationship with Jesus!! And He can do that for you too! It's not about the past as much as it's about from this point forward!

I shared my story, but I see people do this in church. They want people to know how much they give. Or, maybe a church will post how much they are giving to a charity. Maybe, they will even give the Father credit. "I just want to thank God for allowing us to give $10,000 to this charity." I'm just making this example up, because I'm not here to call out a specific person or church. In my example, is that lining up with what Jesus says here in Matthew 6? In my opinion, NO. It's great that you are giving the Father credit, but didn't Jesus say do it in private?

This is a little bit off the topic of what Jesus says here, but I think it falls in line with the discussion about motives. Have you ever seen someone steer a church or try to steer church decisions based on their giving? If you haven't seen it, go to work for a church or ministry, and don't be surprised when you do see it. The mentality becomes – I've given you a large donation – now, here's what I need from you or need you to do. It's sad, but it happens every day.

This falls right in line with what Jesus is saying here. Are you giving for the right reason? Or, are you giving for what you get out of it, whether that be man's praise or man's favors? Give to the Father in secret! Then, patiently wait for your reward!

Prayer…

Jesus starts his discussion about Prayer and Fasting, just like He started His talk about good deeds and giving. He starts with the word "when". When you pray…when you give…when you do good deeds….when you fast. He starts with "when", not "if". Each of these areas is a commandment, an instruction from God. We are told to do them. Jesus assumes the reader has accepted these instructions. These instructions are all actions. Now, Jesus is telling us to do the action with the right heart.

⁵ "When you pray, don't be like the hypocrites who love to pray publicly on street corners and in the synagogues where everyone can see them. I tell you the truth, that is all the reward they will ever get. ⁶ But when you pray, go away by yourself, shut the door behind you, and pray to your Father in private. Then your Father, who sees everything, will reward you."

I think we are starting to see a theme that existed with the religious people of that time. Apparently, a lot of people were doing the right things, but apparently, a lot of them were doing it with the wrong heart. It's looking like these people like to brag about what they were doing to bring credit and glory and praise to themselves. Jesus is saying, the action is good. The heart is wrong.

Is this any different than today? Many do the right things, with the wrong heart. If that is you, please take to heart what Jesus is saying, and make the necessary changes. Keep doing these good things, but get your heart right about why you are doing it and who you bring praise to while doing it.

If you are doing things for the right reason, with the right motives, giving the proper praise to the Father, let this be an encouragement, reminder, and reinforcement to continue! Read this often, and check where you are. Are you still doing it for the right reasons, with the right praise? If so, great! If not, make the changes.

For prayer, Jesus is saying don't stand out on the corner, praying in public, for everyone to see. You'll get rewarded, but again, it's that 'momentary human praise reward', not the 'eternal Father reward' you want. Go into a private place, shut the door, and pray. This is about you having a relationship with the Father, not about everyone seeing how pious (religious) and righteous you are with your prayers. He continues in verse 7 with:

7 "When you pray, don't babble on and on as the Gentiles do. They think their prayers are answered merely by repeating their words again and again. 8 Don't be like them, for your Father knows exactly what you need even before you ask him!"

Jesus says the Father knows your needs. Go to Him, talk to Him in private, tell Him what you need, say what you need to say – but don't babble on and on and on like some people do that want you to think they are some kind of "super" prayer. Please remember, Jesus is reinforcing here that you need to be praying for the right reason. Where is your heart in what you are talking to the Father about?

I think some people are naturally more gifted at prayer than others, but there are times when you just know that a person is trying way too hard to try and pray in a way to impress others.

I also think there is a time and a place for us to get together and pray together. For example, every Sunday morning before service, we have an open prayer time, where anyone in the church can join us to pray for our service. When we do that prayer time, we are asking for the Holy Spirit's presence to be there in our church, we are asking that the Father's will be done, and we are declaring that Jesus will be praised! That is not a private prayer time, necessarily.

There is definitely space if someone wants to go off by themselves to pray, but this is what I would call more of a group prayer time, where we are building unity with prayer to the Father. During this prayer time, I think we can still take very seriously what Jesus is telling us here. When we pray, what's our goal? Are we trying to seem like a super religious, super righteous church that prays a lot? Or, are we coming together as a family in Jesus, to make sure that the Father, Jesus, and the Holy Spirit are glorified? It's up to me as a leader to make sure that it's the second scenario where the Lord is being glorified.

Personally, I don't think that Jesus is saying that a group prayer time like that is bad. Actually, I think this can be a time of allowing people to learn how to pray properly. This can be a great learning experience for everyone. But, if we are not careful, we'll find ourselves in direct conflict with what Jesus is explaining here, if we allow the prayer time to become about us or what we say.

We also need to look at the culture of the people that Jesus was talking to. Not only was He talking to a lot of people that liked to "show off" their religiousness, so to speak, He was talking to a Jewish crowd that would have prayed many scripted prayers per day.

In Luke 11, as well as here in Matthew 6, Jesus gives what we call the Lord's prayer. In Luke, He gives this prayer in response to the disciples, saying "Lord, teach us how to pray." Here in Matthew 6, He gives the same prayer after He warns that we need to pray with the right heart and without babbling on and on.

If we look at the account in Luke 11, why would the disciples ask Jesus how to pray? They were Jewish men that were taught the traditional Jewish prayers from a very young age.

Basically, they were asking Jesus, which of the prayers are important? Out of this, we get what I like to call a "blueprint" of how to pray. We also know it as the Lord's prayer. Jesus says:

"⁹ Pray like this: Our Father in heaven, may your name be kept holy. ¹⁰ May your Kingdom come soon. May your will be done on earth, as it is in heaven. ¹¹ Give us today the food we need, ¹² and forgive us our sins, as we have forgiven those who sin against us. ¹³ And don't let us yield to temptation, but rescue us from the evil one."

Before we break down this prayer, let's address a question. Is this something that you think Jesus just made up on the spot, or is it possible that Jesus was restating something that many of them would already know? Please bear with me for a few discussion points that will answer this question and help us better understand where Jesus came up with this prayer.

The "Jewish" Prayers...

As we stated, the Jewish people had many scripted prayers that they prayed daily. One of those prayers is called the Shema (pronounced 'shmah'). Jesus Himself would have recited this prayer each morning and evening. Shema is a Hebrew word that means "hear", and that is how the prayer begins – "Hear, O Israel; The LORD our God, the LORD is one. Love the LORD your God with all your heart and with all your soul and with all your strength. These commandments that I give you today are to be on your hearts. Impress them on your children. Talk about them when you sit at home and when you walk along the road, when you lie down, and when you get up. Tie them as symbols on your hands and bind them on your foreheads. Write them on the doorframes of your houses and on your gates."

This prayer is basically speaking out Deuteronomy 6:4-9, and the Jewish people would pray this prayer twice a day as a reminder of their commitment to love God and to be obedient to Him, as a reminder of their commitment to teach scriptures to their children, and as a reminder of their commitment to keep scripture in their thoughts at all times. There is more to the Shema, but I'm trying to keep this simple to make a point. This prayer was simply reciting scripture.

Now, let's look at what Jesus says in Mark 12 verses 28-30:

²⁸ One of the teachers of religious law was standing there listening to the debate. He realized that Jesus had answered well, so he asked, "Of all the commandments, which is the most important?"

²⁹ Jesus replied, "The most important commandment is this: 'Listen, O Israel! The Lord our God is the one and only Lord. ³⁰ And you must love the Lord your God with all your heart, all your soul, all your mind, and all your strength.' ³¹ The second is equally important: 'Love your neighbor as yourself.' No other commandment is greater than these."

Do you see what Jesus just did there? He recited the beginning of the Shema. Often, we, as Christ followers, will recite Mark 12, but do we realize that it is a link back to the words found in Deuteronomy 6? To tell us what the greatest commandment is, Jesus recites the beginning of the Shema, which is just reinforcing the Old Testament scripture.

Another example is called the Amidah, which is a series of 18 benedictions. Here's the interesting and important thing about the Amidah. When Jesus's disciples ask Jesus how to pray in Luke 11, they would have asked for a key reason that I mentioned earlier. The Jewish people prayed a lot of prayers per day during that time, prayers like the Shema and the Amidah; therefore, the disciples wanted to know which prayers were important for them to pray as His followers/disciples. Jesus responds with what we know as the Lord's prayer in Matthew 6:9-13, but if you look closely at each section of the Lord's prayer given, it is basically a synopsis of the Amidah!

Maybe you think I just "nerded out" for a minute, but this is important as it helps tie together some important points that we have already made in this book. In Mark 12, as well as in Matthew 6 (and Luke 11), Jesus is not giving us something NEW as many would say. He is simply restating the Old Testament scriptures! In many Old Testament scriptures, it starts with the commandment from God to do this throughout the generations. We are often taught as Christians that the Old Testament was a set of instructions to be used until Jesus came. Then, when He came, He gave us new, better instructions. However, what we see when we dig into Jesus's teachings is that Jesus is often re-emphasizing and re-stating the commandments/instructions of the Old Testament! This is very important for us to understand if we want to be known by Jesus. We'll come back to this point later in the book, so I'm giving you a little bit of a cliff hanger here.

Looking at the Jewish traditions around prayer, which would have been the same exact traditions that Jesus followed, they prayed a lot. They prayed for everything. They prayed before eating. They prayed before enjoying any pleasure in life. They prayed in the midst of misfortune. Now, we are starting to get a glimpse of what Paul meant when he said that we should pray without ceasing in 1 Thes 5:17!

Now, let's look at how the average American Christian prays, in contrast to the prayer style of the Jews of Jesus's time. The average American prayer is quite honestly – selfish. God, please give me this…please give me that…let me get this job….let me get this item…let me get…get…get…. These are selfish individual needs. But, as Jesus is teaching us how to pray, their culture was focused on praising the Father, and they were focused on the needs of the whole people.

It is essential, in my opinion, to lay out all this background information to understand how we should pray as 21st century Jesus followers. We should pray the same way Jesus would have prayed 2,000 years ago!

However, here's our typical daily prayer schedule: pray when I get up, pray a blessing over my food, and pray my "night night" prayers. This is if I'm a good Christian, right? Some can go a whole day or days without praying. That was me for a large part of my life. For the Jewish people, and for Jesus, it was a continual talking to the Father throughout the day, reciting or declaring scripture. AND, it was to praise the Father, while asking for the needs to be met for all the believers and followers of Jesus.

Finally…explaining the Lord's Prayer…

Let's look at the first words of the Lord's prayer: Our Father in heaven. This may seem like a small point, but it's a big point. It does not say "my Father". It says "our Father". The point there is that Jesus was expecting us to pray for the whole of the group, not just our individual and selfish needs. Here's the beauty of this – If we pray the prayer that Jesus says, we get our individual needs addressed without being selfish in our prayer. I want to make sure that was clear. I'm not saying that we shouldn't expect our individual needs to be addressed. We just need to make sure that we aren't praying a selfish prayer. It's back to the heart. I pray a non-selfish (selfless) prayer, and our Merciful Loving Father takes care of my individual needs as well!

Now, let's dig into the blueprint that Jesus gave us for prayer. Something I hear often from Jesus followers – "I don't know how to pray." Well, we can't say that anymore. Jesus has told us where to do it, He has showed us how quick and simple this can be, and He gave us the words that most of us have memorized. What we have memorized may not match the exact translation I used, but I have picked this translation for its simplicity. In other words, we have NO MORE EXCUSES on not knowing how to pray from this point forward. If someone tells us they don't know how to pray, you can teach them now!! If I ask you to pray, or if you want to teach someone how to pray, simply go to Matthew 6:9-13.

There are 31,102 verses in the bible. Jesus tells us how to pray in 4 verses! It's simple. It's time to quit letting satan convince you that you don't know how to pray or that you don't understand.

1. **Verse 9 - Our Father in heaven**, may your name be kept Holy. We are starting with praise to the Father! You are simply recognizing where He is. He is in heaven. You are recognizing His importance and how He is the only set apart, true God. He is Holy. You are reminding yourself that it's a prayer for many, not just your selfish needs (Our Father). Sometimes, as I pray this, I simply say Our Father in heaven, you are Holy. However, sometimes, I spend some time here, telling Him just how great He is! This is a place to worship and to praise the Father, as you begin the prayer. Make this your own. Tell Him things that you

love about Him. You can pray the simple line that Jesus gives, or you can make it more. That's up to you!

One more quick point that we don't want to miss. When it says Our "Father", the Hebrew word is Abba. Abba is most easily described as the English term "daddy". It conveys a level of intimacy of a child calling out to their daddy for help or protection. If you heard a little child yelling Abba, they were calling out to daddy who cared for their safety and well-being. Jesus is telling us that we aren't praying to a 'distant' father. We are praying to our Daddy, Who desires to be close to us, so that He can provide and protect us! Our Father desires to have intimacy with each of us!!

2. **May Your kingdom come soon.** You are declaring that the Kingdom of Heaven WILL come to this Earth, and you are asking for it to come soon. You are asking for the return of Jesus, as the Kingdom comes to Earth.

3. **May Your Will be done on earth**, as it is in Heaven. We are told in scripture that what happens in Heaven can actually happen on Earth. We have to ask for it. That's what we are doing here. Heaven is not just a place that we look forward to going to one day after we suffer through hell on earth. Jesus told us to ask God for His Will to be done on Earth, just like His Will is done in heaven. This is also a great time to remind yourself that this is about God's Will, not your will or my will. This is a point where we are taking out the selfishness. Our world is crazy, getting crazier every day! It's easy to see the chaos of the world, but we

are asking OUR Father to bring some of heaven's peace and joy to the earth.

4. **Give us today the food we need.** For them, food was their daily need. Food and shelter. This is the part that you are asking God to provide what you need to sustain you. Our lives are more complicated now, and we have more needs, but this is where we tell our Father that we trust Him to meet our needs. It says "give us"....not give me. Even when we are asking for our needs to be met, we need to remember that this for the whole, whether that's our family, our church family, or whatever group you are a part of as you pray. This may be where you ask God to give you the car you need to go to work. That doesn't mean it's where you ask for the Lamborghini that you don't need. You are asking the Father to provide for your needs and to sustain you, so that you can help fulfill His Will on earth!

5. **Forgive us our sins,** as we have forgiven those who sin against us. Jesus is telling us that each time we pray, we are to forgive those that hurt us. Then, we ask for forgiveness from Him. We'll dig into this one just a little more in a minute.

6. **And don't let us yield to temptation.** Want a fact of life? Temptation is coming. It's going to be there. You are simply asking God to help you recognize it, so that you can resist it. This ties back to the conversation on taking your thoughts captive. This is a good reminder of that point. You know it's coming, but we are not in fear of it. You know it's going to be there, but you're asking for supernatural help to fight it off.

7. **Rescue us from the evil one** – This is a reminder that satan and his evil angels have one goal. Their goal is to destroy each of us. Their goal is to destroy our purpose and our destiny. But, we have a promise that Jesus came to deliver us from evil! Here, we are asking for God's help to protect us from the evil one…satan.

My hope is that you don't simply memorize this prayer to the point that you get numb to what you are saying. It's a blueprint. Memorize it as a blueprint, and then change up what you say for each point. Sometimes, it might be good to get stuck on #1 for a while, telling our Father over and over and over again just how HOLY He is.

Our Daily Bread…

I know we've gone deep on prayer, but I think it's important to cover two more things. First, let's take a little deeper dive into the meaning of #4. You have probably heard that translated as "give us our daily bread". The word bread is the Hebrew word "Lechem". Like we've stated, it means to ask God to provide for all of your needs. In John 6:35, Jesus says "I am the bread of life". We find the same word, Lechem, there. Jesus is basically saying – I, Jesus, am all you need! As we ask for our daily bread, we are trusting that Jesus is all we need, and He will provide for all of our needs!

As Americans, this point may not hit home as much as it did for the Jewish people that Jesus was talking to. We live in a place where we never worry about eating…we never worry about where we'll get food, for the most part. For the Jewish people, tying their daily need for bread and food to Jesus would have meant more. It would have represented their known need for the Father. Just as we need bread to sustain us, we rely on the creator of the world to provide the Bread of Life to sustain and provide our every need!

Ra ra…

This is the final point that I want to make on the Lord's prayer. When we say "deliver us from the evil one", the Hebrew word used there is "ra", which is a broad term. It means to have physical protection. It means to have protection from being tempted by others to do evil. It means to have protection from one's own selfish evil desires. And, it means to have protection from satan. This simple statement is asking for God's help with the physical and the spiritual things that would destroy our lives.

This is such a simple, short prayer that most of us have memorized, but it's so deep and rich, if we dissect it the way Jesus and His followers would have understood it 2,000 years ago. When we pray, we need to ache for a deeper, more immediate sense of God's nearness and His intimacy. He's not just some distant, unconcerned Creator that lives in a far off place that we call heaven. He cares about us, and He wants to know us!

Giving credit where credit is due!

I would like to give credit to a book for introducing me to some of the deeper concepts that we read about here on prayer. I did not quote directly from the book, but I want to give honor and credit to the authors that helped teach me to look deeper into the Jewish prayers.

The book is called "Sitting at the Feet of Rabbi Jesus: How the Jewishness of Jesus Can Transform Your Faith", by Ann Spangler and Lois Tverberg. This a MUST READ if you want to dig deeper into how being Jewish would have affected Jesus's ministry. It helped spark a desire for me to learn more. I thank God for Ann and Lois's work!

Finally, I would like to thank my son, Peyton Butler. I wouldn't be where I am spiritually without you son! I thank God for you!

Questions and Application for Chapter 10
1. Are you doing good deeds? Who gets the credit, you or God?
2. Are you giving to the Kingdom of God? (to the needy? To ministries?) Is it hard for you to give due to selfishness?
3. If you give to a ministry, do you expect things in return when you give?
4. Do you pray? When you do, do you hope people think you sound good?
5. Did you know how much Jesus re-emphasized the Old Testament? Did you think all His teachings were New and Revolutionary?
6. Do you feel more comfortable that you can pray now?
7. Challenge – Do good deeds! Give to ministry and the needy! Pray without ceasing! Do each of these for the right reason to receive Eternal rewards, not man's approval!

Prayer
"Daddy, thank you for teaching us about the importance of doing good deeds to bring You glory! Thank you for teaching us about the importance of giving to your kingdom! Please expose any selfishness that we need to get rid of that would keep us from taking the time and energy to do good deeds. Please expose any selfishness that we need to get rid of that would keep us from giving. Thank you for teaching us a simple blueprint for prayer. Please ignite a desire in me to want to talk to you more through prayer!"

11

are you telling me that I have to forgive others???

It's conditional…
Have you ever heard someone say that they can't forgive someone? Have you ever heard a Christian say that they can't forgive someone? Unfortunately, most people can answer yes to that question, whether it was from a Christian or a non-believer. As soon as Jesus teaches us how to pray, He gives us a very powerful statement that is CRUCIAL for us to understand.

While covering the Lord's prayer, we briefly mentioned that we would come back to the point where Jesus said to ask for forgiveness AS we have forgiven those who sin against us. He makes it clear there that it's a two-part thing.

Then, immediately after the Lord's prayer, we get two short verses that we need to dig into. In Matthew 6 verses 14 and 15, Jesus says:

¹⁴"If you forgive those who sin against you, your heavenly Father will forgive you. ¹⁵ But if you refuse to forgive others, your Father will not forgive your sins."

Did you get that? Jesus gave us an "if/then" statement two different times. First, IF you forgive, THEN you will be forgiven. Then, He states it again, but with a negative emphasis. IF you refuse to forgive, THEN your Father will NOT forgive your sins.

Here's my concern. We seek out Jesus and believe in Him. We want His salvation. We want His forgiveness. We ask for His forgiveness. We expect His forgiveness. We have someone in our past that we can't forgive or refuse to forgive or don't know how to forgive. We never read these two verses to realize that we have just condemned ourselves.

Does this have your attention yet? Our forgiveness is CONDITIONAL. Jesus did His part. He died, becoming the ultimate sacrificed Lamb, to save us. BUT, we each have a part too! We have to forgive in order to receive that very forgiveness for which He died!

Remember, there is a theme that Jesus has focused on. As we grow closer to Him through obedience, He is trying to mold our hearts to be more like the Father's heart. The Father's heart is to forgive those who believe and obey. He expects us to do the same. He is willing to forgive us; therefore, we have to be willing to forgive others.

In this chapter, we will dig into what it means to forgive. We will dig into how we forgive. If it's conditional to our forgiveness, it's worth taking the time to make sure that we understand.

Let go...

The Greek word that we translate to "forgive" means to send away, or to let go, or to give up a debt. For me, the easiest way to look at forgiveness is to choose the term "to let go". When someone hurts us, we naturally and instinctively carry the pain caused by that hurt. To forgive that person, we are simply saying that we need to Let Go of that pain. Sounds easy, right? Of course it's not easy! It goes against everything in that sinful nature that we carry, if we are to be honest with ourselves. Remember, Jesus has just told us to not seek revenge, and He's told us to love and pray for our enemies. Now, He's telling us to let go of the hurts, pains, bad feelings, hatred, and bitterness that we develop toward someone when we've been hurt. Nobody claimed that this was easy!

Let's make sure that we clarify here that to "let go" doesn't mean that we are telling that person what they did was ok. I think we tend to look at forgiveness as a weakness or as losing. We may still be hanging on to that desire to get revenge. Letting go of the pain that someone caused us seems like we're losing. We lost the battle. We lost our chance to get back at them. They'll think we are "waving the white flag" of surrender.

However, when you begin to understand the true meaning of what it means to forgive, it becomes a beautiful thing. I get it, I probably need to do some more convincing before you see this as a good thing, right? I want to give you two analogies that I think perfectly explain what happens when we don't forgive (unforgiveness). I wish I could tell you where I heard these examples, because I'd love to give those people credit for these analogies, but I've used them for so long, I have forgotten. I guess I'll have to ask them for their forgiveness for stealing their explanations!

Analogy #1 – If you hurt me, and I choose not to forgive you, it's like I drink a bottle of poison, and expect you to die. Who's getting hurt when I drink that bottle, you or me? Obviously, the answer is me! If I don't forgive you…If I don't let go of the pain I have toward you, then I'm the one that continues to suffer, not you.

Analogy #2 – If you hurt me, and I choose not to forgive you, it's like I set myself on fire, hoping you'll die of smoke inhalation. Again, who is getting hurt? In this case, both of us could get hurt, but I'm definitely the one suffering the most impact.

These analogies are similar, and I hope you get the point. When we don't let go of the pain that we are holding toward someone, sometimes we get hurt even more while they experience zero pain. Or, maybe they get hurt a little, but we are still getting hurt significantly more than they are.

We believe a lie from satan that it's not safe or fair or reasonable or warranted to let go of the pain, and we end up having the worst end of the consequences. Maybe, just maybe, the Father knows this because this is what He experiences with us. He loves us so much. If He doesn't let go of the pain we cause Him, He'll suffer more than we do. The one that does the damage usually doesn't care. They are off living their life, not even caring that we are hurt...and that just makes it worse for us. But, do we do that to God as well? We hurt Him when we are disobedient. We hurt Him when we don't want to spend time with Him. But, then, we are off living our lives as if nothing happened, while He suffers.

As we get to know Jesus more and more, and as we allow Him to get to know us more and more, we are continuing to develop the Heart of the Father. As our heart is molded more towards His, we learn that forgiveness is relieving and healing. He desires to forgive us! We should desire to forgive others!

Benefits of forgiveness...

Now that we hopefully understand the importance of forgiving others, we now have to learn how to forgive someone. As we begin to forgive, we begin to heal. How do we heal? Do we heal mentally? Yes. Do we heal emotionally? Yes. Do we heal spiritually? Yes. Do we heal physically? You might be surprised to know that the answer to this is Yes, as well. When you learn to forgive and begin to forgive, every aspect of your life receives healing.

It's probably easy for you to get your arms around mental, emotional, and spiritual healing through forgiveness, but how in the world would unforgiveness affect your physical health? What if I told you that it is a proven scientific fact that unforgiveness leads to bitterness and hatred that can literally manifest into physical illnesses and diseases? Likewise, forgiveness can literally lead to physical healing!

To show you how powerful forgiveness is, I'm actually going to reference a worldly medical article. I normally don't want to include anything worldly into teaching about Jesus; however, I am doing it now to show you that this principle of forgiveness is something that the "world" is beginning to understand, outside of "religion" as they put it. If the world and science can get it, why can't we get it, when Jesus tells us so plainly that we need to do it?

Frederic Luskin, Ph.D. from Stanford Medicine's Center for Integrative Medicine, wrote an article, called "The Art of Forgiveness". Dr Luskin states:

> "Actually, no one has to forgive—forgiveness is a choice. Forgiveness means that we release our suffering over difficult situations; it does not mean we have to put ourselves back into hurtful situations. Forgiveness means that even though what happened is not okay, you can move on and make peace for yourself."

Doesn't this sound a lot like what I stated above? You may be thinking that Dr Luskin wrote this from a Christian perspective. He has already made it clear earlier in the article that he has written this article to be more inclusive than religion or God. He may be a Christ follower, or he may not be. I didn't find that data in the article. The point is that he has written this article to include a bigger audience than just those associated with "religion". Like I stated before, it's a worldly article – that just happens to reinforce biblical principles.

I included this because he is writing to cancer patients, telling them the importance of forgiveness, in their journey for physical healing. He talks about the "grievances or hurts" that cancer patients often have, and he gives them a "worldly" process to forgive because of the healing properties of forgiveness!

Psychology Today published an article on the connection to anger and cancer, referencing studies that go back to 1975. Study after study after study is referenced, tying anger and unforgiveness to cancer. How could this happen, you might ask? Anger and unforgiveness have been shown to suppress the human bodies' natural immune system. I'm not trying to sound too sarcastic here, but maybe, just maybe, there's a reason that Jesus is telling us to not have anger.... and to forgive. Not only does He know the effect it has on our minds (hearts), He knows the effect it will have on our bodies!

In an article from John Hopkins Medicine, titled "Forgiveness: Your Health Depends On It", the author writes:

"The good news: Studies have found that the act of forgiveness can reap huge rewards for your health, lowering the risk of heart attack; improving cholesterol levels and sleep; and reducing pain, blood pressure, and levels of anxiety, depression and stress. And research points to an increase in the forgiveness-health connection as you age."

I think it makes sense to us without question that forgiveness would affect mental, emotional, and spiritual health. However, the moment I mention the physical health benefits of forgiveness, Christians think I'm a 'quack'. It's amazing the "pushback" I receive when trying to counsel someone through forgiveness.

Here's my answer to the "pushback". Jesus said to do it, IF YOU WANT HIM TO DO IT FOR YOU! Even the world gets that it helps our health. Why is it weird for us as believers and followers of Jesus to understand the physical health benefits of forgiveness? That's a question I'll never be able to answer. We believe that God created us with these incredibly complex bodies, which are capable of changing our red and white blood cell count to naturally attack infections and fight off illness in our body. In other words, we believe that God created us with a brain that has the ability to change the chemical structure in our bodies to heal, but we have a hard time getting our arms around how much our emotions can impact our physical health.

Well, I'm not here to argue, although I often do! I'm here to lay out the words of Jesus, and to show you that even the world believes there are positive health benefits to forgiving others. Do it and see what happens!

70x7...

Not only are we supposed to forgive, we are told to forgive many times! We have a scripture that comes later in the book of Matthew, in Chapter 18 verses 21 and 22, where Peter asks Jesus:

"Lord, how often should I forgive someone who sins against me? Seven times?" Jesus replies to Peter, "No, not seven times, but seventy times 7!"

That's a lot! Sometimes, we find it difficult to forgive once or twice, but Jesus says forgive 490 times? So, am I supposed to keep a tally of how many times I've forgiven a person? "Hey, you're at 489... you got one more!" No, that's not the point that Jesus is making. Let's go a little deeper into what Jesus means with that reference.

We have to keep in mind as we read scripture, that there is often a deeper meaning that Jesus's audience would have gotten without Him having to say it. Jesus's teachings are often viewed as revolutionary and new by Christians as we read the bible. But as we've already shown, He was often restating Old Testament principles and instructions to them, and He would often use examples that would mean more to them than it means to us. In other words, He didn't have to say everything for them to "get it".

Back in Genesis 4, there is a story of Lamech, who was a descendant of Cain. Jesus and His disciples would have known this story well, through their study and knowledge of Torah (the first 5 books of the bible). In the story, Lamech inherits his forefather's revengeful, murderous instinct, and killed someone. In Genesis 4, verse 24, Lamech says if Cain is avenged seven times, then Lamech would be avenged seventy x 7 times. In other words, Cain was revengeful, but Lamech was WAY MORE revengeful than Cain.

Now, fast forward to this story in Matthew 18. By referencing "70x7", Jesus was telling Peter that we need to be as eager to forgive as Lamech was eager to seek revenge. Peter and the disciples would have known about Lamech's thirst for vengeance, so Jesus used a well-known thing or term to contrast and to give an example for forgiveness. When He says, "Don't just forgive 7 times... forgive 70x7 times...", they would have understood that He was saying that we need to forgive with the same intensity that Lamech would have used in a bad way with vengeance.

Lamech was vowing a punishment that far exceeded the crime. Jesus was saying that we need to have forgiveness that far outweighs the wrong that was done to us! If we take time to understand this, it also helps us to see how eager the Father is to forgive us!!

We thought Jesus was saying that we just need to forgive a bunch, but He was emphasizing the eagerness we should have in getting to forgive someone! Forgiveness is often hard. We sometimes have a hard time doing it once. I hope this helps to motivate you to have the understanding and eagerness to forgive like Jesus wants us to! The more you forgive, the more Jesus will know you!!

I can't forgive them…they are dead…

One of the biggest misconceptions that people have when we are walking them through forgiveness is that they don't think they can forgive a dead person. That is absolutely incorrect!

Remember, forgiveness is about you letting go. It has nothing to do with the present state of that person. Forgiveness is a "two-way street" with God. You forgive others so that He'll forgive you. Forgiveness is a "one-way street" with the human you are forgiving. You forgive them by "letting go" of what they did that hurt you. You "let go" of the pain. They don't have to be there present for that to happen. In fact, I will encourage you that forgiveness is a very private matter that should ONLY include you and the Father in prayer. In the next section, I will walk you through a practical and easy way to begin the forgiveness process.

Many of us are taught that forgiveness means confronting the person. That is not true. It may involve confrontation in some cases, if you need to set boundaries, but then you may have a whole host of other issues to deal with – like new hurts, new anger, and new bitterness. I think the best way that I can explain this is to give you some examples. I will use one example, but I will change the circumstances to create different scenarios. This list of scenarios is not meant to be totally inclusive, but I hope it helps you get started in the right direction.

I'm going to use a parent and child example. Let's say that you have a 70-year-old man, who has a 40-year-old son. Before you start wondering if I have someone in mind for this example, please know that I have about 100 people in mind for this example. That's why I'm using it! This is an area that satan attacks frequently, and we see this type of scenario over and over in our counseling. Let's say that the 70-year-old man yelled and screamed and physically abused the 40-year-old son, back when the son was a child or a teenager. Now, 20 to 30 years later, the son still carries the hurt, the pain, the memories, and the nightmares. He can still hear the words being spoken harshly over him.

In this example, let's say that we convince the 40-year-old son to forgive his father. He walks through the process and forgives for his own sake (his own forgiveness and his health). Should he go and tell the father that he forgave him? It depends. Let's use the example that he knows that the older man has not changed. If he goes and tells the father that he forgave him, now the father may say all sorts of hateful things, further harming the son. The father may say things that reinforce why the son has held the unforgiveness all this time. That is not a healthy situation. In this example, the son should forgive, but not reach out.

Let's change the example. Let's say that the father has changed. He's received Jesus, and he's a different man. Now, if the son goes to the father and tells him that he forgave him, it can actually drive the father backwards into guilt and shame. If that man, the father, has truly changed, we now run the risk of hurting the father. If the son's forgiveness is dependent on the old man feeling this pain, then it's not true forgiveness, because that involved revenge. And Jesus has told us about that, right?

So, in both those examples, the son needs to forgive – to let go – for his own sake, but I wouldn't recommend him going to His father to tell him about that hurt. In the first example, I'd recommend a boundary of just staying away from the dad. In the second example, I'd recommend pursuing a relationship with the father; however, there is no need to tell the father about the pain. Forgive, and begin to love and build a relationship with that "new" man. Now, if the father asks if the son carries hurt about the past, now, the father has opened up that conversation. If I were the son, I would be honest, and I would tell the father in a loving way that he has forgiven the father. This isn't about hiding the forgiveness. It's about having the wisdom to discuss it or simply just let it go.

There is still another example. Let's say the son hasn't talked to the father in many years. The son doesn't know if the father has changed or not. This scenario is a little more complicated. First, forgiveness is still crucial and needed. The question becomes – does the son reach out to the father? From a forgiveness standpoint, you still have the same scenario as the other two scenarios. Forgive the father....no need to tell him. The question now becomes, do you reach out to see if the father has changed. I think that's an individual decision, and I think it's a case-by-case decision. If you desire to have that relationship, reach out. We have a "born in" desire to have a relationship with our parents. That's in our design. Be ready to love the new man that has changed or to set a boundary and forgive again the old man that hasn't changed. Be careful with this one...

Final scenario – let's say the father passed away. By human nature, people will often think this is the hardest of the scenarios. I disagree. You have eliminated one variable from the equation. I don't mean that to sound as heartless as it does. Forgiveness is still a must, but you don't have to worry about what's next. When it comes down to forgiving, this can be the easiest scenario. We think it's impossible, but it's actually the easiest.

I hope those examples helped you. In the Introduction of this book, I listed out how to contact me if you need help in processing through something like this. I will be happy to help you in your scenario, if God opens up that opportunity. Ultimately, this is between you and the Father in Heaven. I'll do my best to help guide you through.

Let's do this! I'm ready to forgive…

I'm going to give you the most practical and easy way to forgive someone. Many times, we hear that we are supposed to forgive, and we are taught correctly that we are supposed to forgive; however, we are never taught a simple way to do it. That's my goal. I want to teach you the way I do it. God has allowed us to walk hundreds of people through forgiveness. This works, and it's life changing.

Usually, I end the chapter with the application piece, by asking questions and giving a challenge that relates to the topic that was discussed. This one is a little more personal, so I want to walk you through it:

> Take a piece of paper, and write down everyone that you know you need to forgive.
>
> Now, pray this easy prayer. "Father, you are holy. You are merciful, and you are a forgiving Father. I want to forgive anyone that I'm holding unforgiveness toward, because I don't want to block my forgiveness from you. I have made a list of those that I need to forgive, but is there anyone that I have left off my list?"
>
> If you see a face when you ask this, or a name or situation comes to mind, add that name or those names to the list. If it's a person from your past, and you don't remember their name, that's ok. Just write down who it was. For example, "the principle of my school that told me that I'd never amount to anything". I'm making up a random example to show you.
>
> Now, pray this – "Father, who do I need to forgive first on this list?" We are trying to let the Holy Spirit lead us in who we need to forgive, and in what order we need to forgive.
>
> Once you have a face or name, we'll start with that person. If you don't get a clear face or name, start with the person you'd like to. By the way, it may not make sense who God shows you to forgive first. He may show you an easy one to start this process, preparing you for the harder ones later. Or, He may

show you the hardest one first. Or, He may show you someone that you don't even think you have unforgiveness toward. Don't overthink this, just go with what you see or feel or hear.

I'm going to script out how I would forgive them, and I'm going to leave some <u>blanks</u>, to allow you to put in their name and circumstances.

Picture the person as best you can in your mind. I know this is hard when you are trying to keep your eyes open to read. As you do this, and pick up on the process, you can close your eyes to better picture that person in your head as you talk to them.

I want you to say this out loud, just as if you were saying it directly to the person. God has given us vivid imaginations. Please use it here! Start with the person's name, as you picture their face:

"<u>Insert NAME</u>, Today, I choose to forgive you for what you did to me. When I forgive you, I'm not saying that what you did to me was ok, but I'm letting you know that I choose to let go of the pain I'm holding toward you. I'm forgiving you today so that I can be forgiven. Specifically, I forgive you for _____."

(Tell them what you need to say.....be as specific as possible. I forgive you for that time you made fun of me....I forgive you for that time you called me an idiot...I forgive you for molesting me....).

Now, I want you to picture that you are putting all the pain that you have for that person into a trunk. Picture that you are closing that trunk. Now, picture that you are handing that trunk to Jesus. (We don't know exactly what Jesus looks like, but use your imagination!).

Now say:
"Jesus, I'm handing the pain to you, and I'm asking you to cover this pain with your blood, and I'm asking you to take this pain from me. Jesus, Your Word says not to repay evil with evil and not to repay an insult with an insult, but to repay evil with a blessing. Today, Jesus, I ask you to bless **NAME FROM ABOVE**, and I ask you to wash them clean with your blood."

Trust the process...

What should you expect when you do this? Don't expect some magical fireworks display to start going off outside. You may not feel anything at all. However, you started the process! Good Job! The hardest thing to do is to start.

You may have hurt toward someone that called you a name 20 years ago.....or you may need to forgive someone that murdered your relative......or you may need to forgive someone who raped you or molested you. From the smallest of pain to the largest of pain, this process works. I wouldn't lay it out here if I haven't seen the life change that comes from it! I've experienced it myself, and I've walked hundreds through it. (I give ALL praise to the Father!)

You may have to pray this once a day for 30 days for one person that you need to forgive. It's important to understand that forgiveness is a process, and that it can take time. You have to trust the process and stick with it.

The hope is that you'll start to feel more peace toward that person. It will be hard the first time, but as you see results, it actually becomes easier. As you do this, it becomes easier and easier to forgive people.

Most of the time, we are trying to forgive something that happened in the past, maybe many years ago. Now, you'll have a method to immediately forgive someone in the moment or the next day or the next week – so that you don't carry the pain for years. If a person keeps hurting you over and over, there is a discussion there about setting a boundary and possibly needing to get away from that person.

What about you???

Who is the hardest person in the world to forgive? This one can be a tough one, as it is often ourselves. Do you need to forgive yourself? I'll go ahead and answer that for you – YES! Most of us need to forgive ourselves way more than another person. Maybe, the forgiveness is due to our past, poor decisions. Maybe, the forgiveness is due to what we did to others. Maybe, the forgiveness is that we allowed things to happen to us. Whatever the case, YOU may be the hardest person that YOU need to forgive. Please try. Please try.

You use the same process, listed above. Put your own name in the blank, picture yourself, and talk to yourself. This is the one time that you don't have to worry about whether or not it's ok to talk to yourself! You're not crazy – you're trying to heal.

Whether you are forgiving yourself or someone else, please say it out loud. Scripture says there is power in our words. God SPOKE the world into existence. There is something powerful about speaking the forgiveness out loud. Get alone and try this.

Memorize this process and do it often. When you forgive, you get forgiven! When you forgive, you get healing! When you forgive, you get restored peace and joy. When you forgive eagerly, you are learning the heart of the Father, and Jesus is getting to know you well!

12

you hungry yet???

When you fast...
As we continue to process through the Sermon on the Mount, Jesus tells us what our heart needs to look like when we fast. Once again, He starts with the phrase "When you"....when you fast. In Matthew 6 verses 16 through 18, Jesus says:

> [16] "And when you fast, don't make it obvious, as the hypocrites do, for they try to look miserable and disheveled so people will admire them for their fasting. I tell you the truth, that is the only reward they will ever get. [17] But when you fast, comb your hair and wash your face. [18] Then no one will notice that you are fasting, except your Father, who knows what you do in private. And your Father, who sees everything, will reward you."

This is no different than what He has said about Prayer, about Giving, and about Forgiveness – it is to be done in private, where ONLY the Father sees you. And once again, this isn't a "if you fast" discussion, this is a "when you fast" discussion. When you fast, don't do it for attention.

Before we go too far down this path of fasting, let's make sure that we understand what it means to "fast". The easiest way for me to explain fasting is that it means to give up something that is comfortable or something that is normal for you for a period of time. It's not about self-torture, but it should be something that makes you suffer a little, or at least makes you uncomfortable. It is designed to remind you of your dependance on God. It is designed to make you remember to talk to Him more. If I decide to give up something that I rely on every day in my normal schedule, I have to think about my choices. I have to make changes. It may be uncomfortable or inconvenient. Each time I think about what I'm giving up throughout the day, I'm reminded to pray and rely on God for my needs.

Let's take an easy one. I can fast all food for 1 day, only allowing myself to drink water. For most of us, that will cause some problems, right? Not only will I be extremely hungry, but I'll probably be extremely miserable, with no energy. All day, I'll desire to have food. I'll look forward to eating again. I'll have to make conscious decisions not to eat and resist temptation. I can look at that day as a day of total misery, or I can look at that day as a day of dedication and constantly asking for God to get me through the day.

This is a topic that I have never heard taught much in the church, and quite honestly, I don't feel like the church of America, as a whole, puts enough emphasis on the importance of fasting.

The bible doesn't really identify how often we should fast. The bible doesn't really identify exactly what we should fast. The bible does, however, address how we should act while we are fasting. The key is that we don't do it for attention. The religious leaders during the time of Jesus would wear burlap, tear the burlap, and walk around disheveled, because they wanted everyone to know they were fasting and miserable. Jesus is clear. Don't do it so that people will admire you for your fasting. Do it in private for God. If you do it for human admiration, once again, they'll respect you and think highly of you; but, that's all the reward that you'll get. Do it in private, and you get the Father's rewards! That's the reward I want!

Everyone's question about fasting...

I want to address a question up front that I get often. I'll give you an example to answer this question. If you are fasting, and you have to tell someone that you are fasting, did you just lose your reward from the Father? Where was your heart in the situation? Again, this is a heart issue. Why are you fasting?

Literally, one week before writing this chapter, my father came to stay with us, in order to help us with a project. My father lives a little less than 2 hours away, and he came to help us put in a new sink top. A friend at our church gave us a sink top, and we wanted to use it in one of the restrooms in our facility.

Well, I don't have a clue how to install that piece of quartz, or how to cut out for the sinks, or how to plum the sinks. I don't have that skill. My father, on the other hand, can do anything! He's a jack of all trades, and a master at most of them too!

Due to events at our facility which hosts our church, another church, and weddings, we had a limited timeframe to get this project done. So, my dad came to meet our time schedule to help us. It just so happens that it coincided with a 21 day fast that his church had encouraged their people to take part in. So, when he came, he had to tell us what he was fasting, so that my wife would know what to cook for dinner. I have no skill there either, so I had to know what type of fast food to buy him for the lunches, when she wasn't cooking. Did my dad lose his heavenly reward because he had to tell us? I don't think so.

He didn't show up, looking disheveled, bragging about how holy he was. He came to meet our timeframe, to serve us, and he humbly described the circumstances to us so that my wife didn't waste her cooking or get offended if he didn't eat. My argument is that his heart was in the right place. He was fasting for His Father in heaven, but it impacted us as he was serving us.

In fact, it was a witness to me! It reminded me that I haven't fasted since....well, I can't remember when. Fasting is not something that we were taught when I was young, so it's not something that comes natural to me. When I read about it in scripture, or when I hear that someone else is fasting, that's usually when I'm motivated to fast…but it just doesn't come natural.

I believe God used my dad's time of fasting to be a witness to me and my family. It was a reminder that I need to; therefore, I would say that God used his fasting to motivate me. I was also so proud to see my father, worshipping OUR Father, through fasting. It's not that bad kind of pride. I'm using "proud" in the sense of thankful and excited and full of joy that my father is being known by His Father in heaven!! I hope this example helps explain and answer that question.

The Daniel fast…

Throughout the bible, we do see examples of people fasting. Daniel, for example, fasted to set himself apart for the king that he was serving. King Nebuchadnezzar had conquered Israel, due to their disobedience to God. For 10 days in Daniel 1, Daniel fasted from the king's meat and the king's wine. Daniel said that this food would defile him. Daniel, along with Shadrach, Meshach, and Abednego were captured when Babylon overtook Israel. Daniel asked for permission not to eat the meat and wine that was offered to him by the king. Daniel willingly gave up what would have been considered "good eatin'" in order to honor God and in order to set himself apart from the Babylonians. After 10 days, Daniel, Shadrach, Meshach, and Abednego were all visibly more healthy than the other men, and they were allowed to keep eating that way. This may not look like a typical fast, but it was done to honor God, and we know that God rewarded the four men. In Daniel 1 verse 17, scripture says:

> [17] God gave these four young men an unusual aptitude for understanding every aspect of literature and wisdom. And God gave Daniel the special ability to interpret the meanings of visions and dreams.

Later in Daniel, in chapters 10, 11, and 12 – Daniel fasts for 21 days, and God rewards him with a vision about the future. This vision lays out the kingdoms of the future along with end time prophecies that we discuss and use today.

These are just two examples of one man fasting and the rewards that he received from God. I pointed these examples out because you will often hear about the "Daniel Fast" or a "21 day Fast", like I mentioned with my father. Those stem from these scriptures about Daniel. A "Daniel Fast" is typically a vegetable, fruit, and water fast, which is a drastic change and sacrifice from our normal daily intake of steak, chicken, potatoes, cheeseburgers, and fries!

This chapter is not intended to be the "end all" about fasting. The main goal is teach us that we should fast, and when we do, don't do it for attention. Many people will fast when they are praying for something specific, like praying through a job change or some other big life change. Jesus tells His disciples that some evil spirits can only be cast out through prayer and fasting (Mark 9:29). I hope this sparks your interest to learn more about fasting. You want to be known by Jesus? Pray, Fast, and don't do either of those for attention! Do them in private, and receive our Father's reward!

Questions and Application for Chapter 12
1. Have you ever been taught the importance of Fasting?
2. Will you fast, now that you know it's important?
3. When you fast, should you brag about it to others?
4. Challenge – Fast something. You can fast social media for a week, for a month, for 3 days. You can fast sweets for a month. You can do the Daniel Fast for 3 days. You can fast coffee for 21 days. These are just examples. Pray and ask guidance for what you should fast, and do it!

Prayer
"Father, thank you that your Word teaches us that we should fast, and thank you for making it clear that we should do it in private with you! Please give me the strength and wisdom to know when to fast and what to fast. Please help me to seek more of You as I fast."

13

money and stuff... and worry...

Where are you storing your treasures...
I have found that the easiest way to make a Christian mad is to start talking about their money! Jesus has already taught on some "touchy" subjects, up to this point. Now, He's about to really step on some toes!

In Matthew 6, verses 19 through 34, Jesus digs into our money and our stuff (possessions). Just to be clear as we start this discussion, or as Jesus starts His discussion, this is not really about money. Once again, it's a heart discussion. I believe that this is one of the biggest areas of how you can tell where someone's heart is. You can see things like 'selfishness' versus 'selflessness'. You can see 'generosity' versus 'greed'. You can see 'worry' versus 'trust'. How we handle our money and our possessions will show a lot about where are hearts are. It may show us a lot about what we need to work on too! My hope, as we process through these verses, is that we replace the tension that often comes when we mention money – with more peace in understanding where Jesus wants us to put our energy and focus.

If you look up the top things that Americans worry the most about, at the time of this writing, you will get these as your top 4:

1. Money
2. Job Security – which is really about money
3. Relationships
4. Health

In 2020, the fear of death swept over our nation and our world, as Covid19 became a household word that will live in infamy. Even during that year of fear, money still ranked #1, and job security still ranked #2!

Do you worry about money? Have you worried about money recently? Are you worried about your job security? Have you worried about your job security? I hope that you answered NO to all 4 questions, but most of us answer YES to all 4. This conversation from Jesus will be bigger than just money, as it involves all worry. Worry stems from a fear that we won't get what we need. God promises to provide for us. satan works hard to rob our joy and our peace by convincing us that we're at risk daily of not having what we need.

We pray for God to provide our daily needs (The Lord's prayer). Then, we worry that our daily needs won't be met. To put it bluntly – Worry shows a lack of faith! That may be the reason Jesus spends a good bit of time on this topic here in Matthew.

We worry about money.....jobs....relationships....our health.... and a whole list of other things. When a snowstorm is predicted, what happens? Worried people flock to the grocery store and buy milk and bread. Why just milk and bread? Why are those the two things that people run out to get? The truth is that no one knows the answer. There are theories, but no one truly knows. It's just what we do. I live in a state where we get maybe 1 good snow per year that results in maybe 2-to-3 inches of snow. We call 6 inches of snow a blizzard. As soon as the snow is predicted, milk and bread disappear from the shelves.

Something similar happened in 2020. The world was shutting down. We were being told that we'd need a 14-day shutdown.

People went out and irrationally robbed the shelves of toilet paper – again, with no rational reason. Most of our worry is irrational. Better stated, most of our worry is an irrational fear. We covered this in detail in Chapter 7, if you need to go back and revisit.

Psychologists' only answer to why bread and milk fly off the shelves before a snow storm or why toilet paper was in high demand during 2020, is due to the desire for a human to have CONTROL over something that feels out of control. The thought of being pinned in at home creates a fear that we try as humans to control by making irrational purchases. I'm not saying that it's not smart to buy milk or bread or toilet paper, but aren't there some other things you need if you'll be trapped at home? As we have stated many times, Worry is fear. Fear leads to control. Control leads to irrational buying in this case. Anybody ever experience any anger while fighting over the milk, bread, and toilet paper? By the way, psychology now defines "anxiety" as chronic worry. I gave a similar definition in Chapter 7 as we discussed the fear pendulum.

Sometimes, our worries get so big that we begin to act, and then our actions create chaos and shortages of things. But, hey, I'll definitely feel better if I have plenty of bread, milk, and toilet paper, right?

Jesus is trying to bring those worries back to faith in the Father to provide for our needs. Since worry and money are so tied together, that's where He starts. Apparently, things haven't changed much in 2,000 years, and that's why this part of the message stings a little. Humans don't like to be called out for our irrational actions. However, if we are too "worried" to point them out, how will we ever change? How will we ever trust God more?

I know – I got you all messed up about where we are going, so let's get back to scripture! We'll start with verses 19 through 21:

[19] "Don't store up treasures here on earth, where moths eat them and rust destroys them, and where thieves break in and steal. [20] Store your treasures in heaven, where moths and rust cannot destroy, and thieves do not break in and steal. [21] Wherever your treasure is, there the desires of your heart will also be."

If we are going to truly evaluate this, we have to start with our treasures. What drives you to go to work every day? What drives you to excel in your career? What do you do when you have a little extra money? Is your goal to make as much money as you can to buy a nicer house or a nicer car? Or, is work a means to an end for you to pay bills, as you focus on more important things? Is your goal to work hard and get promoted to a better position with better pay? Or, is your goal to show others Jesus while you work? When you have extra, do you give it to charities or to your church or to the needy? Or, do you buy the latest new gadget you've been wanting? Only you can answer these questions, and I'm not looking for your answers. I'm asking you to evaluate where you are with money and your treasures.

The American Dream...
A great disservice to Jesus followers that live in America is the illusion or desire to achieve "The American Dream". I'm about to speak from a level of experience that should earn me a Ph.D. in this topic that Jesus is talking about!

Most of us grow up with the desire to always have more. As Americans, even our most poor are considered among the most wealthy in the world. However, we live with this sense of never having enough. If we have a car that functions and gets us where we need to go, we want a better, nicer, newer, fancier car. If our house or apartment is big enough and sufficient for our needs, we constantly find ourselves wanting something bigger and better. If the newest iPhone or iPad or Apple Watch comes out, we find ourselves wanting the latest and greatest. We seem to live in a perpetual state of never having enough, and then we call it chasing "The American Dream", like it's a good thing. In fact, I see a new mini storage facility being built almost continuously in the area where I live. We have so much stuff that we have to rent space to keep our stuff! I know some people need mini storage space to facilitate moves and to allow transition, but many people just have one or more to store their stuff! That's ridiculous....but I have to admit...I was one of those people.

It's really a consumer based mentality that can never be satisfied. It's a lust for more – a lust for what we don't have. We are all guilty of this at some level. Here's the illusion – One day, I'll reach the point of having all I need, and I'll be done. Can you trust me when I say that day simply doesn't ever come? It never will come!

We have two major problems. We have fear that we won't have enough, coupled with lust for what we don't have. (Glad we have already covered both of those topics in detail!)

We think that money will satisfy the fear and that money will satisfy the "wants" that we have. But, money is just a false sense of security. Having more stuff is a false sense of satisfaction.

Here's the reality for most. The more money we have – The more money we spend. Then, the more stuff we accumulate, the more problems we have. Then, we begin to rely on credit (loans, credit cards, etc) to satisfy what we can't really afford. Now, we have snowballed into something that really generates worry! How can we pay the bills??

As I eluded to back in Chapter 3, I was not only chasing the American Dream, I caught it! I had everything I ever wanted. I had way more than I ever needed. There was no material thing that I wanted that I didn't buy or have. Here's the problem. I was empty. I had no joy. I had no peace. I had no self-control. I had earthly treasures that would make anyone jealous, but I just had new worries.

Can I maintain this level of sales at my job each year to sustain this lifestyle? Also, I had so much stuff, but it seemed like every time I wanted to use that new stuff, there was a problem. Something was broken or wouldn't start. A friend of mine would say things like "more money….more problems…". He was absolutely right! I was more stressed and worried when I had all the money that I could ever ask for than I am now, when I'm having to trust God day to day for finances.

This is what Jesus is talking about in verses 19-23. Your earthly treasures feel good at the moment you buy them. It satisfies a lustful need in that moment. However, it's a false sense of security. Those earthly treasures waste away, and they cause you more problems. They don't sustain the things that matter.

Heavenly treasures on the other hand satisfy two needs. I gave up everything, sold everything, to pursue this new lifestyle of helping others find and follow Jesus more closely. I don't want to give you the illusion that I don't have anything left, but I'm trusting vehicles that average 170,000 miles on them. I used to buy and sell cars so often that I literally went almost 10 years at one point, without ever needing an oil change! For those that are not mechanically inclined, you typically change your oil every 3,000 miles. I didn't keep brand new cars for the first oil change. That's how ridiculous life was.

The Eternal Dream!

Now, I have all the fruits of the spirit listed out in Galatians 5. Those are Jesus rewards that I have here on Earth. Part 2 is that I'm building up heavenly treasures! I had the American Dream; however, the best decision I ever made (besides loving Jesus) is that I gave up the American Dream for my new Eternal Dream!

I used to wake up every day, wondering what deal I could close to make money or what thing I could buy. Now, I wake up, wondering who I get to talk to about Jesus today! Who do I get to invest in to help them get closer to Jesus? Yes, I still have to pay the bills, and I work to do that, but work is now a means to an end, to provide for ministry. I'm living the Eternal Dream!!!!

This entire Sermon on the Mount discussion has been about our hearts. Don't miss what Jesus says in verse 23 – "Where your treasure is, there the desires of your heart will also be." Where is your treasure?

I know many Christians that have a false sense of security in earthly treasures. I know very few that truly find their security in heavenly treasures. I've said this many times – Let me see where you spend your money and where you spend your time, and I'll tell you where your treasures are!

During this conversation, I never said you couldn't have nice things. It's not about the stuff. It's about where you put your time, energy, and money. If you put zero time, zero energy, and zero money in heavenly investment, then there is a good chance that you're

100% investing in earthly things. If you put a little money and time into heavenly investment, that's better. However, Jesus is expecting us to put our time, our energy, and our financial resources into serving and following Him! Then, He'll sort out what we need for earthly sustainment.

Colossians 3:23 – great motto!

Let me give you an example. I mow yards and do landscaping on the side – to make ends meet for our ministry. When I'm out there mowing a yard, I do the best I can for that customer at the best price I can. I'm working hard, and I'm making money. My mentality while I'm working is based out of Colossians 3:23:

> "Work willingly at whatever you do, as though you were working for the LORD rather than for people".

As I'm working, I'm praying/talking to God, or I'm thinking about who to help, or I'm listening to a sermon. I'm working as if I'm working for the LORD, not the customer. I do the best job I can. Then, if I get to talk to them, I do my best to get into a "Jesus" discussion with them. I promise that I'm not trying to brag about how holy I am. I'm trying to make a point that I can store up heavenly treasures while mowing yards. No matter your job, no matter your circumstances, you have the choice to approach life from an earthly perspective or from a heavenly perspective. I've done both, and I am here to tell you – HEAVENLY IS BETTER! I would say that I am living proof that heavenly is better!

The problem that I think we have to be honest about is this – There are many Christians, walking around claiming the love and salvation of Jesus, while building up way more earthly treasures than heavenly treasures. You want to be known by Jesus, make sure your time, energy, and money reflects more toward storing up heavenly treasures!

One Master at a time...

In verse 24, Jesus says:

[24] "No one can serve two masters. For you will hate one and love the other; you will be devoted to one and despise the other. You cannot serve God and be enslaved to money."

I don't think Jesus could be any clearer here. He is telling us that either money will be your master or God will be your master. You can't have both being your master. Again, He didn't say you can't have money. He said it can't be your master.

He says something really interesting here, that is worth noting. He said you will hate one and love the other. These are strong words that we need to PAY ATTENTION TO! If you love money, you hate God. If you love God, you hate money.

I had those moments when I loved money. It was my master. It drove my decisions, my actions, and my time. I never thought that I hated God. But, when I began to self-evaluate and realize just how much I loved money, I realized that meant I only had one option for God – hate. When I realized that, it was EASY to make the change in masters!

Now, God is my master, and money is my slave, so to speak. I try to do everything I do for God because of my love for Him. I make money when I work, and I use that money to fund the things that help build His Kingdom!

Do you see how that changed in my life? If I can focus on that, and make that change, then anyone can. I promise you that. I really, really loved money. Now, I really, really love God! It takes self-evaluation as you read these scriptures to make the change. It takes being honest with yourself about who is your master. For me, the thought that loving money meant that I hated God – that was all the motivation and incentive I needed to make the changes I needed to make!

Just like I stated previously, show me where you spend your money, your time, and your energy, and it'll be a clear answer to whether money or God is your master. If your thoughts are consumed with how to make money, what to buy next, what item you need to be less stressed, what entertainment you need (sports, etc), or what vacation you need next, then I know your answer….and it's not a good one. I didn't say we should never think about those things. The key word that I used was "consumed". If it's all you think about to the point that it is what motivates your daily life and drives you, it's a problem that needs to change.

On the other hand, if your thoughts are consumed with how you can Love God, how you can love your enemy, how you can serve your boss, how you can worship God with a song, how often you pray/talk to God, and how you can use the money you make to better the Kingdom of God, then I know your answer....and it's a good one! God is your master.

This one is a tough self-evaluation, but I never want to be in the place again where I hated God, due to my love of money. I don't want you to be there either! So, you want to be known by Jesus? Don't find yourself guilty of having money as your master!

The Rich Young Ruler...

In this discussion and self-evaluation, you have to be careful that you aren't trying to do some "Jesus" stuff while also letting money be your master. You can do both, and fool yourself. Remember, in my example, I tithed big checks to the kingdom, fooling myself that everything was ok.

Let's look at the rich young ruler in Matthew 19, verses 16-22:

"Someone came to Jesus with this question: "Teacher, what good deed must I do to have eternal life?" 17 "Why ask me about what is good?" Jesus replied. "There is only One who is good. But to answer your question—if you want to receive eternal life, keep the commandments." 18 "Which ones?" the man asked. And Jesus replied: "'You must not murder. You must not commit adultery. You must not steal. You must not testify falsely. 19 Honor your father and mother. Love your neighbor as yourself.'" 20 "I've obeyed all these commandments," the young man replied. "What else must I do?" 21 Jesus told him, "If you want to be perfect, go and sell all your possessions and give the money to the poor, and you will have treasure in heaven. Then come, follow me." 22 But when the young man heard this, he went away sad, for he had many possessions."

That story was about a real man. That was not a parable to make a point. That was not a hypothetical situation. That was real. This man did all kinds of good things. He kept the commandments, the instructions we have been discussing. But, when Jesus said, "go and sell your stuff and follow Me" – the young man went away sad, because he loved his possessions. Jesus knew that this man was a slave to his possessions. Many Christians have read this story over time, and they think that Jesus is telling everyone that they need to sell everything they own to follow Him. That is not what's going on here. Jesus did not tell everyone they have to do that. He told that specific man, because He knew that man's heart. He knew that man loved his possessions more than eternal things. He was doing lots of good things – good actions – but his heart was not in the right place when it came to who His master was.

We can mask our thoughts and motives to those around us. We can do all sorts of good, God loving actions. Those things can make us look holy. But, Jesus cares about your heart behind the actions.

How big is that needle?

There are two more verses that immediately follow to round out this discussion. Matthew 19, verses 23-24:

> ³Then Jesus said to his disciples, "I tell you the truth, it is very hard for a rich person to enter the Kingdom of Heaven. ²⁴I'll say it again—it is easier for a camel to go through the eye of a needle than for a rich person to enter the Kingdom of God!"

This is the single verse that Jesus used to change my life. I realized that I was the rich young ruler, and I realized that I lived under an illusion of having eternal life with the Father, when I was more likely destined for eternity in hell.

Maybe you didn't have all the possessions I had. Maybe you don't have all the possessions that the rich young ruler had. BE THANKFUL! Be thankful that you didn't reach the point that he and I reached. However, I think some "believers" have reached the same point with fewer possessions. Jesus is making it clear in

Matthew 6 as well as here in Matthew 19, that the kingdom is the opposite of the world! The world says find success in money, and find success in possessions (stuff). The kingdom says find eternity in giving up worldly stuff!

By the way, many people wonder – exactly how could a camel ever go through the eye of a needle? Does that mean it's impossible to have money and get into the kingdom? Let's look at what the term "eye of the needle" meant back during the time of Jesus. Immediately, we think about a very small sowing needle, with an eye so small we can barely get thread through it, much less a camel, right?

Back in the time of Jesus, the entrances to the cities would have had large gates. They would have also had a smaller passage that people could walk through. Now, as people were trying to enter or exit on foot (walking), these smaller passageways meant that they wouldn't have to open the large gates. This smaller passageway was called "the eye of the needle". Camels have a hard time bending down. The eye of the needle entrance was shorter than a camel. It was not impossible for a camel to kneel down and get through the eye of the needle, but it was very difficult. You would open the big gates for a camel to freely walk through.

Jesus was saying – "It's not impossible…but it is much harder to get that camel through the smaller passage way" – called the eye of the needle. I hope that helps you get a better picture of what Jesus is saying.

Do we really trust God?

As soon as Jesus is clear about not letting money be our master, He immediately transitions to the discussion about worry. We tackled part of this discussion at the beginning of this chapter, but this is where Jesus gives us the scripture. In Matthew 6 verses 25-34, Jesus says:

^{25} "That is why I tell you not to worry about everyday life—whether you have enough food and drink, or enough clothes to wear. Isn't life more than food, and your body more than clothing? ^{26} Look at the birds. They don't plant or harvest or store food in barns, for your heavenly Father feeds them. And aren't you far more valuable to him than they are? ²⁷ Can all your worries add a single moment to your life?

²⁸ "And why worry about your clothing? Look at the lilies of the field and how they grow. They don't work or make their clothing, ²⁹ yet Solomon in all his glory was not dressed as beautifully as they are. ³⁰ And if God cares so wonderfully for wildflowers that are here today and thrown into the fire tomorrow, he will certainly care for you. Why do you have so little faith?

³¹ "So don't worry about these things, saying, 'What will we eat? What will we drink? What will we wear?' ³² These things dominate the thoughts of unbelievers, but your heavenly Father already knows all your needs. ³³ Seek the Kingdom of God above all else, and live righteously, and he will give you everything you need.

³⁴ "So don't worry about tomorrow, for tomorrow will bring its own worries. Today's trouble is enough for today."

If money is your master, worry will torment your life. When we worry, it shows a lack of faith in God. Jesus said it, not me! In verse 30, He says "Why do you have so little faith?" We need to understand this concept and understand the importance of not allowing worry and fear into our lives.

It's a pretty simple formula. We have two options. Put your faith in money, let it be your master, and you will worry about everything – OR – Put your faith in God, let HIM be your master, and trust Him to provide for your every need! Choose Option B, and live worry free! Choose Option A and hope your camel can crawl through the eye of the needle!

I've lived them both. I'm not trying to be redundant and constantly repeat myself. I want you to learn from my mistakes, I want you to find hope in my testimony, and I want you to have the love for the Father and the faith in the Father that I have! For me, once I made the decision to switch masters, it was an instantaneous change. My faith grew immensely in a moment.

As I told people that I was leaving my career, leaving the position I'd spent 14 years building, and leaving the money, everybody thought I was experiencing a mid-life crisis or a mental breakdown. It definitely was not a mid-life crisis because I was ready to sell all the things that you buy in a mid-life crisis. I always made the joke that you buy a Porsche in a mid-life crisis, but I was selling mine! I also knew it wasn't a mental breakdown because I was experiencing a peace I had never felt before in my life.

However, people didn't understand it. I would tell them, I read this scripture, and I'm changing my life. I know God told me to leave my career, so I'm leaving immediately. They couldn't understand the radical change. I would get questions like "what are you going to do Jason?" My answer was "I don't know. So far, God has only told me to leave my career and pursue Him with all my heart. I trust Him to tell me later what's next." People thought I was insane. I had a wife and two young children. Those who didn't think I was crazy, thought I was being irresponsible.

Here's the thing. These were Christians that had such a hard time accepting that I was actually making changes due to scripture. These were Christians that didn't understand how I could have the faith to leave with no plan. These were Christians that didn't understand the peace I was experiencing from finally being obedient. These were Christians that questioned why I would follow what Jesus clearly said to do!

I felt like God had warned me with the story in Matthew 19 about the rich young ruler and the eye of the needle. And, I simply trusted what Jesus said here in Matthew 6. It was time for God to be my Master, instead of money. If I say that I trust scripture, I then had to trust these things where Jesus says "Don't worry, God will CERTAINLY take care of you."

Not only did Christians not understand, many of them turned against me. Instead of understanding my desire to please God, they accused me of abandoning them. Many of them ridiculed me. I was told by one man (a Christian) that he wanted the old Jason back.... the "sinful, fun" Jason.

I had complete peace about my decision, but utter confusion at some Christians responses. I even had my pastor tell me that he thought it was a mistake for me to leave my career! He was more interested in my big checks than he was about my life change, my newfound devotion and faith, and my eternity.

This was before social media dominated our communications, so the best way for me to tell everyone what I was doing, was to send emails. I emailed over 1,300 coworkers and clients, telling them why I was leaving. In that email, I was honest. I was vulnerable. I told them that I couldn't cheat people to get money anymore, and that I couldn't serve money any longer. I told them that I was a hypocrite. I told them I had lied to many of them. I asked for forgiveness as I made these changes. I told them about my newfound trust in God to take care of me.

Christians bashed me. Christians questioned me. Christians made fun of me. BUT – I had a few atheists tell me that they were inspired by my faith in a God that was so strong I would give up the worldly success to follow Him. Yes, you read that correctly. Some atheists were more accepting of my decision than some Christians were!

This example is what is wrong with Christianity today. There are too many people trying to serve both masters. There are too many Christians that think it's weird that I'd obey scripture and have that much faith. There are too many Christians that justify the worry in their lives instead of realizing that it exposes a lack of faith.

I'm living proof that this sermon from Jesus can change your life. I'm concerned that many Jesus followers look like the rich young ruler – do the right things – but ultimately are not willing to give up the master that is money. I'm passionate about trying to convince you to live out what Jesus says here. It's the most fulfilling thing I've ever done. I'm still learning every day. I'm still making changes. Living out the instructions that Jesus gives us here is the best decision I ever made. What will you do with it?

Seek the Kingdom first…

Jesus gives a simple instruction to us here as we finish this chapter. He says:

"Seek the Kingdom of God above all else, and live righteously, and He will give you everything you need."

Do you believe Jesus? Do you believe Him when He says this? Do you trust His word, or is it just a cute phrase we quote on social media to make ourselves look holy?

I love how Jesus wraps up this discussion on money, worry, and faith. He says:

"Don't worry about tomorrow….tomorrow will have its own issues…."

How many of us spend each day worrying so much about the next day or week or month or year or bill to be paid – that we miss the beauty and joy of the present day?

By the way, I am not trying to claim that I have no worries. I have thoughts enter my head every day that I have to take captive. I have to teach those rebellious worrying thoughts to obey Christ. This is about living a lifestyle of making God your master and trusting Him.

You want to be known by Jesus? Go against the world's norm. Make God your master, not money. Let your faith outweigh your fear and worry! Seek the Kingdom of God above ALL ELSE! Live in obedience to Jesus, and trust the Father to take care of your needs!

Questions and Application for Chapter 13
1. When you make a decision in your average day, do you stop and think about if that decision is creating an Earthly treasure or a Heavenly treasure?
2. Where are you spending your time, your energy, and your money? Earthly or Heavenly things?
3. Who is your master? God? or Money?
4. If it's money or if you don't know, what changes do you need to make to change your focus? (hint: your thoughts go a long way here!)
5. Does worry dominate your thoughts? Do you trust God to meet your needs?
6. Challenge – Take an inventory on where you spend your time, energy, and money. If God is not in any of those or in only a few, change one thing to bring Him into more of your daily life. Remember, you can do the same action with a different motive and change your master.

Prayer
"Father, thank you for warning us with scripture about where we store up our treasures. Please show me the areas that I need to change in order to make sure that I'm storing up heavenly treasures instead of earthly treasures. Father, please help me to make sure that You are my master. Help me to use money to be the tool that helps me do and fund ministry – instead of it being my master. Father, thank you for Your promises that tell me that You will provide for us! I bind up all fears in Jesus's name and tell worry to leave, as I build more trust in You!"

14

judging...

Can we judge? Should we judge?

Should a Jesus follower judge someone? Should a Jesus follower stay away from judging someone? Does it depend on whether the person being judged is also a Jesus follower? Is it our choice if we want to judge? What if the answer to all those questions is – Yes? We will dig into these questions as we explore what Jesus says about "judging others".

Jesus starts out in Chapter 7 of Matthew with 6 verses of instruction on judging others. In verses 1 and 2, He says:

"Do not judge others, and you will not be judged. ²For you will be treated as you treat others. The standard you use in judging is the standard by which you will be judged."

Let's start by defining the word "judge", and then, we'll break down these two verses. The Greek word used here means to "pronounce an opinion concerning right and wrong". We typically associate judgment with only pointing out the wrong. But, to truly judge, you have point out the right and the wrong. We don't mind getting told what we've done right. We usually love that part! It's the part about hearing wrong that we don't like. Maybe, pride is getting in the way of us hearing that negative truth that we need to hear. That's an important place to start this conversation, so I'm going to say it again – true judgment involves being told if you are RIGHT or WRONG....not just wrong.

With that understood, let's get to the verses. Many times, we'll hear or read the very first part of verse 1 and stop. "Do not judge others." There it is – black and white – don't judge others.....Jesus said it.....right? However, it changes things if we add in the part after the coma – "Do not judge others, and you will not be judged." Now, we start to see that we have a choice, and our choice affects us equally. Let's keep reading – "For you will be treated AS you treat others. The standard you use in judging is the standard by which you will be judged."

Jesus is giving us a choice. Choice 1 – Don't judge, AND you won't be judged. Choice 2 – You can judge, and you will be judged the same in return. That's how I can answer three of those questions above as Yes. We'll get to the fourth question in a moment.

When we read scripture, we need to read the scripture before and the scripture after to get the full context. We can't just pick a verse out and use it, without understanding the full context of what's around it. In this case, we can't just pick half a verse, and use it.

If we look at the context of this sermon, it's about changing your heart away from the world's standard to gain a heart that is molded by the Kingdom of God. It's about doing the right thing for the Father, without doing it for man's attention and praise. It's about changing how we treat others as we gain the heart of the Father. If we allow all these things to happen, we will naturally not want to judge as much.

Human nature – the sinful human nature – allows fear to turn into control, remember that discussion? Well, there is that other aspect that comes along with that control that we mentioned back in Chapter 7. As a reminder, at times, we may try to control our fears by being critical of others. Let's say that I have a fear that I'm not doing enough for God. Instead of taking that thought captive, binding up that fear, and teaching that thought to obey Christ as I do my good works for the Father – it may just be easier for me to start looking for what others ARE NOT doing for the Father. Now, I'm better than them, right? That's being critical and being judgmental.

You are probably noticing that Jesus is asking for a lot of self-reflection, as we follow Him. Self-reflection or self-evaluation is hard. I have often said that most of us have "blind spots". Let's make sure you know what a "blind spot" is. Let's say you are driving down the highway, and you want to switch lanes. You check your mirrors, and you see no cars. However, every car has a "blind spot", where the mirrors can't see a specific area. If there is a car in that blind spot, you won't see it, no matter how hard you look in that mirror.

It's the same for us. You may be willing to look in the mirror and self-evaluate. First of all, if you are willing to look in the mirror, good job! However, sometimes, no matter how hard we look, we just can't see what's actually there in our "blind spot". In the car, you can turn your head and physically look in that blind spot to see if a car is there before changing lanes. With our self-evaluation, sometimes, the only way to see the "blind spot" is to ask someone else to help us. That someone needs to be a trusted friend, who is also a follower of Jesus. Don't pick a critical, insecure person for that job. If you do, you'll get more criticism than just what's in your blind spot!

Back to judging. I'm trying to make a point that this is not a simple "yes or no" question, in terms of should we judge or not. Jesus says – "Judge at the level that you want to be judged". That's the best way for me to sum up verses 1 and 2. For me, if I am steering off the Narrow Path that we'll talk about here in a few verses, then I want another believer to lovingly point that out to me (judge me lovingly), so that I can get back on the right path. At the same time, if I'm struggling with fear, and I'm praying to shed it…to bind it up…to replace the lie with a truth, I don't need someone to tell me that I'm struggling with fear. I know it, and I'm actively working on it.

So, often, I will ask someone if they want help in an area. I'm ok with being judged, so I don't mind judging others. However, I want to be judged in loving manner. In other words, I want someone to judge me for my own benefit, not because they are critical. If that's what I want, then I better do my judging of others in a loving, non-critical manner as well!

Hypocrisy...

Jesus goes a little deeper in the next three verses. In verses 3 through 5, He says:

> ³ "And why worry about a speck in your friend's eye when you have a log in your own? ⁴ How can you think of saying to your friend, 'Let me help you get rid of that speck in your eye,' when you can't see past the log in your own eye? ⁵ Hypocrite! First get rid of the log in your own eye; then you will see well enough to deal with the speck in your friend's eye."

Jesus just changed gears to talk about hypocrisy. This is not the first time that we've addressed hypocrisy in this book.

If you are going to judge, make sure you have dealt with that same thing in your own life before you attempt to give your opinion of right or wrong to another person. Make sure you have corrected the wrong in your life before pointing out the wrong in someone else's life.

Let's give an example. Maybe, I see that someone is struggling with fear. I'm being very general here. It's just fear. I can see the fear, but I can also see that they don't recognize it. It has become a blind spot for that person. Now, I decide to tell them. I'm ok with being judged if I'm dealing with fear, so I decide to tell them what I see.

HANG ON! I missed a step!

Before I confront them lovingly about what I see, I have to stop and ask God: "Father, is there any fear that I need to deal with before telling them what I see in them?" It may be that I have a lot of fear that I'm not seeing! I'm quick to see this little fear that they have, but I'm not seeing some big fears that I have. That's a log in my eye versus a speck in their eye. In other words, my issue is bigger, and I need to deal with that issue before going and telling someone about their smaller issue.

It's hypocritical to help someone else, even with the best intention, if you are not willing to look at your own problems first. Think back to what Jesus has addressed often in this sermon. Many times, the discussion has been: "Don't be a hypocrite. Don't tell someone else to do something that you aren't doing yourself". It's the same thing here. "Don't be a hypocrite. Don't judge someone's 'wrong' if you aren't willing to address your 'wrongs'"!

Don't cast your pearls to pigs…

What about that fourth question that we still haven't answered. Should a Christian judge a non-believer? We will talk about what Jesus says about this, and then we'll tackle a passage of scripture from Paul that reinforces what Jesus says here in verse 6. Jesus says:

"Don't waste what is holy on people who are unholy. Don't throw your pearls to pigs! They will trample the pearls, then turn and attack you."

Don't waste what is holy on people who are unholy. Jesus just told us that it is Holy to judge someone, if it is done accurately. Do you see that? When you judge someone the right way, with the right heart, after self-evaluating and getting your own problems dealt with, you are doing a HOLY thing! Judgement is holy. Most Christians believe a lie that Christians should not judge. However, here, Jesus says it's Holy to judge. It's about your heart. The heart of the Father involves judgement. He is going to judge our good things and our bad things. That judgement will determine our rewards, here on Earth as well as in eternity with Him. The Father is Holy. His judgement is Holy. When we judge the correct way, with the correct heart, it is Holy!

Jesus is telling us that our judgement is to happen between believers. Jesus expects us to want to be more Holy every day. To be holy means to be set apart, remember? Judgement should happen from Christ follower to Christ follower. That fourth question that I started the chapter with was – Does it depend on whether the person being judged is also a Jesus follower? The answer is Yes. If they are a Jesus follower, then you have a choice on whether or not to judge. If you judge, do it without hypocrisy. Deal with your own stuff first. But, if they are not a Jesus follower, don't judge. Don't waste your holiness on people who are not holy.

Paul has something to say about this too...

Paul shed some light on this topic, as well. In 1 Corinthians 5, Paul tells us about a man that is involved in sexual sin WITHIN the church. Paul is chastising the church for allowing this sin to carry on. You can read 1 Corinthains 5 to get the full story, but I want to focus on what he says in verses 12 and 13, which are at the end of the chapter. He says:

"*12* It isn't my responsibility to judge outsiders, but it certainly is your responsibility to judge those inside the church who are sinning. *13* God will judge those on the outside; but as the Scriptures say, "You must remove the evil person from among you."

Paul says don't judge those outside the church (non-believers), but we are supposed to judge those inside the church (believers). Now, there is a key phrase here that he says – "judge those inside the church who are sinning". Many Christians say that we shouldn't judge within the church, but Paul clearly says right here that we should judge when it involves sin. In this case, the person would not repent, so Paul told them to kick the man out of the church. But, if a person is a non-believer, it's God job to judge that person. Sometimes, I think we get that backwards. We judge the non-believers, and then say don't judge the believer. Paul says very clearly that we DO judge the believer, but we leave the non-believer to God for judgement.

I want to emphasize again that "sin" is what is to be judged. I'm about to give a ridiculous example to make a point. If you don't like my beard, you are free to have that opinion. Before you "judge" my beard, here's an important question – Is my beard a sin? If Yes, judge me, tell me. If No, it's just your opinion. There is no judgement to happen. You can share your opinion with me. If you do it in a critical and non-loving manner, then I can decide if I want to judge your fear or not (being critical due to a fear is a sin...). Make sense? Whether Jesus is talking about judgement, or Paul is talking about judgement, both are talking about judging sin in our lives. That is an important point to make. Judgement is for sin, not opinions...

Stringing pearls together...

Now, Jesus says a catchy phrase – "Don't throw your pearls to pigs." You may know this phrase from a different translation that says "Don't cast your pearls before swine". This deserves some explaining.

First of all, pigs are nasty, filthy, biblically unclean animals. God's people were instructed not to eat them, which makes sense when you realize they are Earth's natural garbage disposals, full of parasites that often make us sick! Not only are they nasty, but they were used as sacrifices to other gods. You either believe in God (big G) or you believe in a god (little g). You either believe in the Almighty God, who has many names (like Elohim, Yahweh, I Am, etc.); or, you believe in a false pagan god. Jesus is using the term pig here to designate someone that believes in a false god. By the way, some people today will say they are "agnostic", meaning they don't believe in anything. That's not an option. You either believe in God or a god. That god may be yourself....

What about the term "pearls"? That term would have meant something to the Jewish people that Jesus was speaking to, and I think it's worth explaining.

Teachers (Rabbi's) would use a technique in teaching called "Stringing Pearls together". The easiest way to explain this is to say that they would string together scripture from different parts of the Bible to bring the old scriptures to life for those they were teaching. You have to remember, they didn't have this nice pretty bound book that we know as the Bible back then. They had what we know as the Old Testament only. When Jesus is talking, there is no New Testament. It hadn't been written yet. The "Old Testament" that they did have wasn't put together neatly into a book. They would have had a scroll for Torah (first 5 books...the books of Moses). They would have had scrolls of the Prophets (Isaiah, Jeremiah,

Ezekiel, etc). They would have had scrolls of the other "Writings" (Psalms, Proverbs, Ecclesiastes, etc.).

As they taught, a Rabbi would link the words from the Torah - to words from the Prophets – to words from the Writings. They considered all the words to be valuable, like Pearls. As they strung together these pearls, it delivered a better, deeper message. A pearl by itself is valuable, right? As you put more and more pearls together, it creates a necklace or a bracelet. That necklace or bracelet is worth more than a single pearl. This is what it means to say "they would string pearls together". It was more valuable to string scriptures together to make a point.

For example, back in Matthew 5, when Jesus gave the blessings (covered in Chapter 3 of this book), these are actually references to Isaiah as well as references to the Psalms. As Jesus said these words, He was stringing pearls together to remind the crowd of God's promises to rescue His faithful followers. He was stringing pearls together to make one major point: GOD IS FAITHFUL. Our Father cares for us, and He will bless us if we seek Him even when life is painful and hard. Once again, I'll state that Jesus wasn't preaching some new revolutionary idea to them. He was stringing together pearls that they would understand.

Now, maybe it's a little more clear why the Old Testament is still relevant and important to read. Also, hopefully it's more clear why it is SO DANGEROUS to throw out the Old Testament. As you read the Old Testament scripture, you can be thinking about how it is linked to other Old Testament scriptures. Not only that, but you can think about how those are linked to a New Testament scripture! Now, scripture is becoming more and more alive! It's becoming more valuable, as we learn to string the pearls together!

Another example is found in Mark 1:11. As Jesus is baptized by John, the scripture says [11] And a voice came from heaven (the Father's voice): "You are my Son, whom I love; with you I am well pleased."

We read this, and it sounds like a great statement from the Father toward Jesus; however, it's much deeper! God is stringing together pearls with this simple statement. He is actually tying together three Old Testament scriptures:

1. Psalm 2:7 – You are my son
2. Gen 22:2 – Take your only son and sacrifice him
3. Isaiah 42:1 – Here is my servant, my chosen one in whom I delight. I will put my spirit on Him, and He will bring justice to the nations.

When the people around heard this voice from heaven, they would have recognized how the Father Himself strung the pearls together of these 3 scriptures to describe Jesus, and His purpose. This is My Son, who will be sacrificed for all! Psalm 2 and Isaiah 42 are both prophecies about the Messiah! The story in Genesis of Abraham being willing to sacrifice Isaac is a prophecy about the Messiah! God is stringing the pearls together for the people. The words in the prophecy "my Spirit will be poured out on Him" are being brought to life as God pours out His Spirit on Jesus right then and there! This does not change what we read in Mark 1, but it helps us go deeper into an understanding of what God was proclaiming in that statement at Jesus's baptism. The Father, with an audible voice, was declaring that Jesus is the Messiah!! The Jewish people would have understood this!

When Jesus calls Himself the Good Shepherd in John 10, He is stringing together pearls from Psalm 23, about a shepherd's comfort, with passages from Isaiah 44, Psalm 78, and Ezekiel 34, where the King is called the Shepherd. As King and as Shepherd, Jesus came to bring comfort and ultimately power, like a king. When Jesus calls Himself a shepherd in John 10, He is laying out His identity as the Messianic King – the future ruler of God's Kingdom. This would have really meant something to the listeners of this time. Some would have been shocked. Some would have been excited. Some would have thought this was scandalous and blasphemous!

One last example of this. In scripture, Jesus often called Himself, the "Son of Man". Jesus calls Himself the Son of Man over 80 times in the Gospels of Matthew, Mark, Luke, and John; but what does

He mean by that? To get our answer, we have to go look at a pearl in Daniel. In Daniel chapter 7, Daniel is explaining a dream that he had, and in verses 13-14, he says:

> [13] "In my vision at night I looked, and there before me was one like a son of man, coming with the clouds of heaven. He approached the Ancient of Days and was led into his presence. [14] He was given authority, glory and sovereign power; all nations and peoples of every language worshiped him. His dominion is an everlasting dominion that will not pass away, and his kingdom is one that will never be destroyed."

This passage in Daniel would have been universally understood as a reference to the coming Messiah. As Daniel prophecies through the dream, the high point of the dream is when this humanlike figure enters God's throne room, He is crowned, and He sits down on the throne to reign. This was considered one of the most important Messianic prophecies in all of scripture back in this time. This "Son of Man" referenced was far more than just a man – He was divine. Jesus's audience would know each time that He called Himself the Son of Man, He was referring to this scripture in Daniel – and He was declaring Himself the Messiah by simply using that term!

These pearls would have made some listeners respond in Awe! He just claimed to be the Messiah! Some listeners would have responded in Anger! He just claimed to be the Messiah! They would have either believed He was the Messiah, or they would have thought He was blasphemous. There was no middle ground. As Jesus teaches, He expects you to pick a side - worldly versus kingdom – money versus God – earthly reward versus eternal reward.

Now, back to the scripture at hand. Does this help you understand the deeper meaning when Jesus says "Don't waste what is holy on people who are unholy. Don't throw your pearls to pigs!"?

The final words here – "They will trample the pearls, then turn and attack you."

We are supposed to tell people about Jesus. If they believe, that's great! Teach them, disciple them, correct them, judge them (if you are dealing with your own stuff…). However, if you tell someone about Jesus and they refuse to listen, don't keep wasting what you have that is holy on them. You have pearls! They are pigs. Don't cast your pearls before the pigs! Jesus says, they will trample your pearls (your scripture). Then, they will turn and attack you. He is giving a warning. If someone doesn't want what you offer them in the redemptive, salvation story of Jesus, they will trample on you, and attack you.

Some of us experience this with social media. On social media, I only post things about Jesus. That's my criteria. If it glorifies Jesus, I post it. If it has nothing to do with Jesus, I don't. Once in a while, I will post something about Jesus, and a random stranger (that we coincidentally call a 'friend' on Facebook…) will attack what I say. In the past, I would defend my point, standing up for Jesus! In doing so, I learned what Jesus meant here in this scripture. I also learned what it means in Proverbs 26, verse 4, where it says "Do not answer a fool according to his folly, or you yourself will be just like him."

They can get vicious in how stupid they think I am. If I engage in that argument, I become a fool as well. That person made up their mind before responding to my post. Now, I just tell them I'm praying for them. That usually doesn't end well either! This is a small example of how the pig has turned on me to attack.

There's a lot in these verses! Judge at the level you want to be judged. It's your choice. Don't be hypocritical if you decide to judge. Make sure you are taking care of your own problems. Make sure that you are judging SIN, not what you dislike. Don't throw your pearls before unholy pigs. Finally, REMEMBER, as you judge, don't forget to tell them what they are doing right! Understanding and applying all this will get you known by Jesus!

More Credit due!

Once again, I would like to give credit to the book "Sitting at the Feet of Rabbi Jesus: How the Jewishness of Jesus Can Transform Your Faith", by Ann Spangler and Lois Tverberg. I learned a tremendous amount from their book, and it has greatly influenced the discussion about the "pearls" in this chapter.

Questions and Application for Chapter 14

1. Have you been taught that we should never judge anyone?
2. Now that we have explored this scripture/teaching, are you ok with being judged? Are you ok with judging others?
3. Will you allow others to lovingly help you with your "blind spots"?
4. Can you judge without being critical?
5. Will you stop and evaluate your own issues before judging?
6. Will you remember to do some GOOD judging by telling others what they are doing right?
7. Challenge – Stop and think before you judge someone. Answer some questions. Is this sin that I'm judging? Am I ok with them judging me back? Am I telling them the good and the bad? Have I cleaned up this area in my life before I judge this area in their life? Am I doing this with the right heart of love?

Prayer

"Father, thank you for this scripture that gives us clear instructions on judgement. Thank you that You judge our bad to correct us. Thank you that You judge our good to reward us! Please help us to judge others the way You would judge us. Help us to lovingly help others when we see their blind spots. Help us to not be hypocritical when we see sin. Help us to self-evaluate our sins before we point out other's sin."

15

More good info on prayer!

Is it ok to ask God for something more than once?
A person once told me that when we pray, we should ask God one time for something, and that's it. If you ask more than once, it shows a lack of faith. Well, I believe the words of Jesus disagree with this statement completely!

In Matthew 7, verses 7-11, Jesus says:

⁷ "Keep on asking, and you will receive what you ask for. Keep on seeking, and you will find. Keep on knocking, and the door will be opened to you. ⁸ For everyone who asks, receives. Everyone who seeks, finds. And to everyone who knocks, the door will be opened.

⁹ "You parents—if your children ask for a loaf of bread, do you give them a stone instead? ¹⁰ Or if they ask for a fish, do you give them a snake? Of course not! ¹¹ So if you sinful people know how to give good gifts to your children, how much more will your heavenly Father give good gifts to those who ask him."

Jesus starts with – keep asking – keep seeking – keep knocking. Jesus is saying the exact opposite of it being a lack of faith. He says – BE PERSISTENT in your prayers. Now, I think it's worth noting, based on the theme of this sermon, that we are asking for things that further the Kingdom of God, not selfish things. If I keep asking for a Lamborghini or a Ferrari, I don't think Jesus is telling me that's what I'll get if I'm persistent. However, if I'm asking for things that will help the Kingdom of God, He says our prayers will be answered.

That doesn't mean that our prayer will be answered exactly the way we think it should be. Remember, in our prayers, we are supposed to pray in accordance with God's will. As I ask for something, I'm trusting in God's will. Let me give you an example. Let's say that a very close friend is deathly sick. I pray for them to be healed. If I'm praying for someone to be healed, that's not selfish – I'm praying on behalf of that person, trusting that God's healing power can restore them! Maybe I pray about this multiple times a day for weeks. Then, my friend dies. As humans, we would be quick to look at a scripture like this, and say – "Why didn't my friend get healed? I kept asking God to heal that person, just like Jesus said…" Well, maybe death was the ultimately healing, because that person's suffering is done, and now that person is with Jesus! It's not the way I wanted them to be healed, but it was God's will, and their suffering is done.

Many times, I'll pray for something, and it does not turn out the way I want it to, or the way I think it should. Then, maybe even years later, I'll look back and THANK GOD for not answering the prayer I ask for the way I asked it. In other words, I prayed, and God answered. He answered and provided a better scenario than I prayed for because He knew the need and situation better than me.

That's what it means to have faith when you pray. Pray for your need, pray for it if often and persistently, and then trust God for the outcome no matter how closely it resembles what you asked for as an outcome. We need to apply this to everything we pray for. God knows our needs better than we do!

Shameless persistence....

Jesus used an example in Luke 11 to reinforce this same thought about being persistent in our prayers. In verses 5-13, Jesus says:

⁵ Then, teaching them more about prayer, he used this story: "Suppose you went to a friend's house at midnight, wanting to borrow three loaves of bread. You say to him, ⁶ 'A friend of mine has just arrived for a visit, and I have nothing for him to eat.' ⁷ And suppose he calls out from his bedroom, 'Don't bother me. The door is locked for the night, and my family and I are all in bed. I can't help you.' ⁸ But I tell you this—though he won't do it for friendship's sake, if you keep knocking long enough, he will get up and give you whatever you need because of your shameless persistence.

⁹ "And so I tell you, keep on asking, and you will receive what you ask for. Keep on seeking, and you will find. Keep on knocking, and the door will be opened to you. ¹⁰ For everyone who asks, receives. Everyone who seeks, finds. And to everyone who knocks, the door will be opened.

¹¹ "You fathers—if your children ask for a fish, do you give them a snake instead? ¹² Or if they ask for an egg, do you give them a scorpion? Of course not! ¹³ So if you sinful people know how to give good gifts to your children, how much more will your heavenly Father give the Holy Spirit to those who ask him."

Jesus tells us in verses 5-8 that if we "bug" God long enough on a prayer request, He'll answer out of our shameless persistence. Then, the rest of the verses (9-13) sound almost identical to what we are told in Matthew 7!

Good gifts from a good Father!

Whether we are looking at Matthew 7 or in Luke 11, I love the analogy that Jesus uses to describe our Father. He ties it back to us as parents. If we are good people, we want to give our kids good gifts, right? Many of us go overboard in this area and completely spoil our kids.

Jesus tells us that if we, as sinful humans, like to give good gifts to our kids, how much more would a PERFECT FATHER want to give to those that ask!

In the story in Luke 11, we see something interesting that is a little different at the end of the story. In Matthew 7, it says our Father will give good gifts to those who ask. In Luke 11, it says our Father will give us the Holy Spirit!

As we implement what we are learning here from Jesus in the Sermon on the Mount, and as we grow closer to having the heart of God, we learn to ask for the more important things instead of the selfish things. We should want the Holy Spirit to guide and direct every decision and action that we do! If we are getting more and more of the Holy Spirit, then our selfish requests will naturally begin to disappear.

It's not only about being persistent, it's about asking for the right thing. We need to pray that our Father will give us good gifts, and we need to pray that our Father will give us more and more of the Holy Spirit. What else could we want other than the Spirit of the Living God living inside us to direct everything that we do??

You want to be known by Jesus? Be persistent in your prayers, and receive more and more of the Holy Spirit!

Questions and Application for Chapter 15

1. Are you persistent in asking God for your needs?
2. Are your requests selfish or Kingdom focused? (For example, you can ask for $ from God. Are you asking for money for your selfish material desires? Or, are you asking for money to help further the kingdom?)
3. Do you trust God for the outcome of your prayer request WHEN the outcome doesn't match exactly what you asked for?
4. Do you want more of the Holy Spirit? Do you see that as a good gift?
5. Challenge – Pray and pray often. Pray with persistence. Ask for Kingdom things. Trust God when the outcome doesn't seem to match the prayer request. Sometimes, it's years before we realize just how much the outcome did match the request! Don't reject the GIFT of the Holy Spirit!

Prayer

"Father, thank you that You made it so clear that you want us to be persistent! Thank you that you don't get tired of hearing from us! Please give us the faith to trust the outcome of our prayer requests, even when it makes no sense at all to us. Thank you for answering prayers with answers that line up with Your Will, not my desires. Father, we pray for Your Will to be done in all things! Thank you for the gift of your Son Jesus! Thank you for the gift of the Holy Spirit! Help us to receive the gift of your Son's salvation, and help us to receive the Power that comes from the gift of the Holy Spirit!"

16

The build up before the BIG VERSE!

The Golden Rule...
As we process through the Sermon on the Mount, we are getting very close to the verse that drove me to write this book. I'll be honest – I'm excited to get there. We only have a few more topics to cover before hitting the big verse!

In Matthew 7, verse 12, we get a short and simple verse, but if we can learn to live out this verse daily, this will make many, many things fall into place, in terms of our lives matching up to the Kingdom of God (the Heart of the Father and His Will!).

Jesus says:

"Do to others whatever you would like them to do to you. This is the essence of all that is taught in the law and the prophets."

This is a well known verse, that almost every believer knows, and we call it the Golden Rule. It's simple, but so important. Treat others the way you want them to treat you. What if we lived each day, treating everyone around us the way we would want them to treat us? What would that do for our lives? What would that do for those around us?

Jesus does NOT say treat others the way they treat you. That's the way many of us live out this command. If you are rude to me, then I'll be rude to you. We live with the "eye for an eye" mentality that Jesus has already talked about. He says the opposite – He says treat others the way you WANT them to treat you.

Now, let's apply that. If someone is rude to me, I treat them with kindness – because that's the way I would want them to treat me. If someone hurts me, I forgive them – because that's the way I would want them to treat me. If someone yells and screams at me, I speak to them with calm and encouraging words – because that's the way I would want them to treat me.

Such a simple verse, but do we do it? Jesus says – "this Golden Rule is the essence of all that is taught in the law and the prophets". Remember, Jesus is the only human that has walked this earth that truly understands the intent of God's instructions. Jesus sums everything up with this one statement – "All of the Father's instructions come down to how you treat people." Remember also that Jesus has told us that the greatest two commandments (instructions) are: 1) Love God 2) Love Humans. If we love God, we obey God. We do what He says to do. He says to Love Humans. Treat them the way we would want them to treat you. Boom! That's it! Easy formula! Why is it so hard?

It's hard because of the sinful nature in us. We want the success of the world. We want God's blessings with very little work done on our part. We want to rewrite all God's instructions. We want to be angry at times. We want what we can't have, whether it's sexual or some other selfish desire. We want to go back on our word sometimes (or often). We want revenge. We want to get back at our enemies. We want the praise of humans. We want to look holy, without the heart change. We want money and stuff. We want to point out other people's flaws without self-reflecting. We want our desires to be met without talking to God persistently. All I did there was walk through a negative aspect of each topic that Jesus has just walked us through with the Sermon on the Mount.

If we could just do one thing – one thing – If we made every decision toward people, based on how we would like them to treat us, we would fulfill God's perfect instructions. So simple, yet so hard!

Jesus has taken the time to tell us how to correct our sinful nature that makes this one instruction so hard. We should want Kingdom success. If all our thoughts are based on how to be Kingdom minded, we will treat others better. We should want to do whatever it takes to have our Father's blessings. We should want to know God's instructions, and we should work hard to follow them. We should never want to be angry, because we don't want others to be angry with us. We should be satisfied with what God gives us. We should want to be selfless, not selfish. We should want to keep our promises, because we would want others to keep their promises to us. We should never want revenge, because we wouldn't want someone to seek revenge on us. We should love our enemies, because we would want our enemies to love us. (If we did this part right, we wouldn't have enemies…). We should want the praise of the Father, not the praise of humans. We should constantly seek heart change, so that we can be more set apart (holy). We should want heavenly treasures, not earthly treasures. We should each be looking at what we need to change. If each of us did that, we wouldn't have to judge each other. We should beg for more time to talk to God to tell Him our desires. All I did there was walk through a positive aspect of each topic that Jesus has just walked us through with the Sermon on the Mount.

The instructions are easy, actually. Defeating our human sinful nature is what is hard. Want to be known by Jesus? Go against your sinful nature, and treat EVERYONE the way you would want them to treat you, no matter how they actually treat you!

The Narrow Gate…

In Matthew 7, verses 13 and 14, Jesus says something that ought to grab our attention! He says:

> ¹³"You can enter God's Kingdom only through the narrow gate. The highway to hell is broad, and its gate is wide for the many who

choose that way. ¹⁴ But the gateway to life is very narrow and the road is difficult, and only a few ever find it."

Basically, Jesus is saying that it's easy to follow our sinful nature….all the way to hell; but, it's actually going to take some work to get into God's Kingdom. I think this is an area that we need to be careful to make sure that we don't go to extremes. On one side, you have this mentality that you can do whatever you want, ask for forgiveness, and slide right into heaven, even though you have lived a very worldly life, full of selfish, sinful activity (greazy grace extreme). Then, we have the opposite extreme where we have a mentality that we have to work our way into heaven, and it's very hard to be good enough (religion extreme).

Both of these are scripturally wrong. It does take hard work to enter into the Kingdom. I want to be clear. I'm not doubleminded, and I didn't just use a conflicting statement. You can't work your way into heaven – FACT. Grace is a gift we can't earn. Ephesians 2 verses 8-9 state this:

"⁸ God saved you by his grace when you believed. And you can't take credit for this; it is a gift from God. ⁹ Salvation is not a reward for the good things we have done, so none of us can boast about it."

Now, let's balance this. Jesus just laid out a lot of areas that we need to work on in our lives to change from our natural, born in, sinful nature. Then, he says the gate to the Kingdom of Heaven is narrow, and the road is difficult.

There is a difference between good works and hard work (or difficult work). Good works are something that you are expected to do as a believer – to show your living faith. Your good works don't save you. The FREE GIFT of Salvation saves you. Living a life, worthy of entrance into the Kingdom, is hard…it is difficult. Why is it difficult? Because many are comfortable living their worldly, sinful life, and it feels like hard work to live with a kingdom mentality. The difficult part is not so much about the works, it's about the decision to be different than your sinful nature. It's so difficult that only a "few" will make the decision to change. Only a few will make the decision to live out what Jesus has laid out in this sermon. When Jesus says "only the few", the Greek words used here mean "only a few". I know you were expecting some profound difference of words or meanings like we often get when we go to the Hebrew or Greek meaning; however, in this case, Jesus literally means only a few. No where (to my knowledge) is it defined in scripture what "a few" means. Is it a 1,000? Is it 10,000? Is it 10 million? Is it 10 billion? We don't know. We only know that the term "a few" means a small # or a small percentage.

There is a reality that Jesus is telling us that we have to make some changes in our thoughts – in our hearts. We have to kill off the sinful nature of our flesh, by allowing Jesus to transform our thoughts and actions. Doing good things doesn't earn us heaven, but not changing our sinful nature will earn many hell.

This may scare you or motivate you. If you have learned to fight fear and you are making changes to align your heart with the Father's heart, it shouldn't scare you. It should motivate each of us to try EVERY DAY to find the areas that still need work in our lives.

If you are living a 'greazy grace' life, then maybe we need a little scaring....to scare us away from hell!

Only half will get in???

In Matthew 25, Jesus gives a parable about 10 bridesmaids (or 10 virgins in some translations) that are waiting for the groom. When the groom finally comes, only 5 are ready. 5 are allowed into the wedding feast, and 5 are denied entry. 10 people thought they were getting into the feast, but only half were ready. What does that mean for the church? Does that mean that half of the church that thinks they'll get in will be left out? Does that mean that half of the people that call themselves believers are actually believers?

I can't define how many a few is, and neither can you. We don't know if half of "believers" are really believers. But, there is an interesting consistency between this story and where we are getting to in Matthew 7. In Matthew 25, verse 11, the groom (which represents

Jesus) says to the 5 bridesmaids that were not ready – "But he called back, 'Believe me, I don't know you!'"

Doesn't that sound just like a verse that we are getting to?? I believe that Jesus is giving us a clear warning to be prepared. This motivates me to be ready! Does it scare you? Does it motivate you? If you have never taken these instructions from Jesus seriously, are you ready to? Are you ready to evaluate each area of your life and make changes where you need to? I want to be one of the few. I want to be one of the 5 bridesmaids (believers). And I want you to be one of the few! And I want you to be one of the "half" that gets in!

Jesus has laid out the groundwork of what He expects. If you've never been taught the importance of it, now you have. Now, you know what He expects. Now, you know what to evaluate. Now, you know what you need to change. Now, you know what's at stake.

Do you want to be one of the few? Do you want to be at the wedding feast with Jesus? I hope you said YES to both. Following His instructions is not hard. Making changes once you know what needs to be changed is not hard. Killing off your sinful nature is difficult. That's why the Gate is Narrow; that's why only a few get through it.

Actions speak louder than words...

We have one more section of scripture to cover before hitting the crucial scripture that started this journey, and it has to do with the fruit of prophets.

In Matthew 7, verses 15-20, Jesus says:

[15] "Beware of false prophets who come disguised as harmless sheep but are really vicious wolves. [16] You can identify them by their fruit, that is, by the way they act. Can you pick grapes from thornbushes, or figs from thistles? [17] A good tree produces good fruit, and a bad tree produces bad fruit. [18] A good tree can't produce bad fruit, and a bad tree can't produce good fruit. [19] So every tree that does not produce good fruit is chopped down and thrown into the fire. [20] Yes, just as you can identify a tree by its fruit, so you can identify people by their actions."

Jesus says that we will produce fruit, and it will either be good fruit or bad fruit. We can determine if that person is producing good fruit or bad fruit, by watching their actions. There is an old saying that our "actions speak louder than our words". Jesus is telling us – watch what someone does (action), and you will know their fruit. It's easy to learn the knowledge to talk a big game, but our actions show if we are living out that knowledge. Many of us know people that can quote scripture with the best of preachers, but we don't see that same scripture lived out in their daily lives. That hypocrisy is what I believe turns off many people from wanting to hear about Jesus. If the world hears the message, but then does not see us act on it, why would they want the bad fruit that we are producing?

Be careful not to get caught up in what people say before you watch to see what their actions do. Good versus bad fruit is about the actions we see. You and I can memorize word for word what Jesus says in the Sermon on the Mount. What good does that do if we are not living it out? Very little. In fact, it can produce much damage while producing very little good.

We should all get our arms around the fact that we are being watched. Someone is watching you. I don't mean some creepy stalker! If you are a parent, your spouse and kids are watching you. Your coworkers are watching you. The world is watching you. As a pastor, I know that people are watching to see if my actions line up to the words that I speak. I also know that my two sons are watching. I'm more concerned with what they see day to day at home. If they see us gossiping for example, we have given them the right, the authority to lovingly tell us what they see. It's not about being perfect in living out scripture, but it's about being willing to change when you know that your thoughts and actions don't line up to scripture. It's about allowing the Grace of Jesus to cleanse you as you make mistakes and learn and grow and change.

We've gone full circle with this discussion and sermon. It starts out with quit worrying about your actions, change how you think. Then, it transitions to how your thoughts will begin to change how you want to act. Then, it ends with the fact that our actions show our fruit. If it's good fruit, great! Heart change has happened, and we are living a life, worthy of being known by Jesus. If it's bad fruit, we better make some changes before we get chopped down and thrown into the fire! Jesus wants us to change how we think – so that it changes how we act – so that it changes any bad fruit to good fruit! Nobody wants a rotten banana to eat, right? However, if you have ever had a fresh fruit, pulled straight off the tree, there's nothing better or sweeter to eat! That's what Jesus wants – He wants us to be good, fresh fruit, that is sweet for the world to eat! I guess we can be sweet and salty!

Beware of the ole false prophet...

We need to make sure that we do not miss some very important instructions here from Jesus. He has given us a warning here that we need to spend a little bit of time on. He says "Beware of False Prophets who come disguised as harmless sheep but are really vicious wolves".

Have you ever heard the term "a wolf in sheep's clothing"? That's what Jesus calls a False Prophet. A false prophet is defined as one, who is acting the part of a divinely inspired prophet, but utters falsehoods under the name of divine prophecies. That was the fancy definition. I'll try to give it to you in everyday language. A false prophet is someone who claims to have a message from God, but they are lying. It's not from God, and it does not line up with scripture. It may be from satan, or it may be from their own thoughts... but it is NOT from God.

To understand what a prophet should be, we can look to the prophets in the bible. This list is not designed to be comprehensive, but here are some common, household names: Isaiah, Elijah, Elisha, Jonah, Jeremiah, Ezekiel, Daniel, Hosea, Zechariah, John the Baptist, and John the disciple. If you look at what is common between these men, they all followed the same pattern. They took scripture, measured it up against the actions of the people of their time, and warned their people to repent and turn back to God before disaster happened (God's punishment). God used many prophets to warn Israel for hundreds of years before allowing Israel to be captured, due to their disobedience. God was so merciful....so loving that He sent these men over and over to warn because He did NOT want to punish His people. He does not delight in punishment. God delights in mercy!

Other than warnings, we also have prophecies about those who would be coming in the future, as well as prophecies about events that would happen in the future. For example, Isaiah prophesied about the Messiah, Jesus. Not only did Isaiah tell about Jesus, but he prophesied that Jesus would be rejected by God's people, which would allow Jesus to be offered to the Gentiles. Daniel prophesied about the coming antichrist and the tribulation period. John, the disciple, prophesied about the return of the Messiah, the antichrist, the false prophet, the tribulation, the millennial reign, and the New Heaven and New Earth. Many prophecies have happened, but there are many still yet to come. Prophecy is very important. When Jesus came, and His life, His suffering, and His death matched up to the prophecies of the Old Testament Prophets, the people would've had a reason to believe that Jesus was the Messiah. However, many rejected Him because false prophets declared the Messiah would be a warrior king.

This is a great example from the past that I can use to describe a false prophet. A true prophet like Isaiah said to look for a Messiah who would be beaten and bruised. If you read Isaiah 52, starting in verse 13 and continue through all of Isaiah 53, it tells us that Jesus would be beaten to the point that His face would not be recognized. It tells us that His appearance would not be beautiful or majestic. It tells us that He'd be despised and rejected. It says He would be pierced, beaten, and whipped. He would be oppressed and treated harshly. He would be a lamb, led to slaughter. His life would be cut short. He would do no wrong, but be buried like a criminal. He would be put in a rich man's grave. He would die for our salvation.

If you knew those words of Isaiah, and then you saw Jesus come along, you would recognize that EVERY word that Isaiah spoke about the coming Messiah – EVERY WORD OF IT – happened to Jesus! That was true prophecy.

Now, let's look at the opposite. That story is not exactly what people wanted to hear. People would rather hear about a conquering

King, like David. So, false prophets would come and mislead people, telling them not to worry – A Messiah is coming that will conquer and defeat the Romans!

Jesus came, and He fit 100% what Isaiah said….but too many people listened to the false prophets, thus denying Jesus as the Messiah. Do you see the damage of false prophets? What would you have rather heard? "Your coming king will be beaten and die" – OR – "Your coming king will reign and defeat your oppressors"? Of course, the people wanted the second option, not the first. Because they listened to the false prophets, they missed Jesus.

Same for us today. God has prophets. satan has false prophets. The battle is still the same today, as it was a few thousand years ago. God's prophets warn. satan's prophets mislead with false hopes and false securities to try and draw us away from God.

If you hear prophecy today where they use scripture to warn (and it truly lines up with scripture), they are, by definition, true prophets. However, if they give any information that contradicts scripture, or if they give timelines or events that don't happen, they are, by definition, a false prophet. We tend to be like God's people 2,000 years ago. We'd rather hear a "feel good" hope from a false prophet than a true "not feel good" truth from a real prophet. We have to be careful, and that's why Jesus warns us. Our sinful nature will easily follow the false prophet because it's a message we want to hear. We have to be ready to test the prophet's message to see if it's true and to see if it lines up with scripture.

In the Christian movement today, the fastest growing area is in prophecy. Here's the problem. Many of them are false prophets, like we are warned about here in Matthew 7. Many of them will "prophecy" great and elaborate things over your life, but then those things never happen. Often, they'll use elaborate and ornate language that gives you something that feels really good about your future, but it never happens. I'll give you an example. In 2022, a proclaimed prophet gave 25 prophecies over two speeches. They were oddly specific prophecies about revival in specific countries, about worldly political things that would happen, and about a peace treaty from a specific leader at a specific time. NONE OF THOSE THINGS

HAPPENED. By definition, that man is a false prophet – he is a wolf in sheep's clothing – and Jesus said Beware of him! He said that each of his prophecy's came from divine inspiration from God, but he gave false hopes that didn't happen. That means he lied. His fruit was lies and false prophecies – bad fruit! Here's the problem. This man is seen as one of the great and upcoming "prophets of God" right now.

By the way, to tie this back to the beginning of Matthew 7 – if satan can convince us that we aren't supposed to "judge" others, then you might think I'm sinning by judging this prophet. However, I am willing to be judged if I give a prophecy, so I look at his bad fruit and call him a false prophet, just like Jesus warned about.

False prophets are very dangerous. Jesus said they are like vicious wolves. Why are they vicious? When their prophecies don't come true, it creates doubt for the Jesus followers who were misled by them. It almost always hurts that person's faith. It creates worry and fear, which separate us from God. This is an important point for Jesus to make as He's getting ready to end His sermon. Jesus is saying that we need to each be constantly asking God what we need to work on. We need to hold others accountable for what they say or do in God's name, or we will be misled into the hands of a vicious wolf and not even realize it. It's hard enough to find that Narrow Path and Gate. It's hard enough to fight off our sinful nature. Now, we need to be careful that we aren't following a human leader that will lead us astray and away from God. Our human church leaders should be doing everything they can to get us through the narrow gate. False prophets confuse, create doubt, and steer us down the wider path to hell!

Again, I'll re-emphasize. Most of the prophets of the bible were warning people about destruction if they didn't turn back to God. They weren't fortune tellers, like many of the prophets today. Every day, I seem to hear about a prophet having a dream or a vision about the future that promotes something big that never happens. I have friends who send me prophetic visions regularly. I don't read or listen to them with negative expectations. However, I'm trying to look at their fruit.

If I hear the same dream happening over and over (or similar dream), but nothing in that dream actually happens as predicted, that's bad fruit. By definition, we need to quit listening to them; however, I often get a lot of pushback when I point this out to people. They think I'm being negative or judgmental, when I'm just trying to live out what Jesus says. This is just one example of what Jesus means when He says "it's difficult". Even believers will be deceived. I watch Christians defend false prophets frequently. Jesus warned us, but we are getting fooled by the vicious wolves!

If their prophecies are aligned with the bible and come true, listen to them! If their prophecies are not aligned with the bible and don't come true, get away from them! They are wolves! There is a reality that we live in a time that self-promotion is at an all-time high. Many prophets are promoting themselves on social media without producing good fruit. It's all about them. It's all about building their "brand". It's all about money.

Now, contrast that to prophets in the bible. They were all about God, not themselves! Isaiah didn't create his own ministry called "Isaiah the Prophet" and promote it on the most popular social media platform of the day. It was quite the opposite. Prophets were despised. Prophets didn't have many friends. It's not popular when you are telling others they need to repent! That's one of things that is wrong with the church today – It's not popular to warn and tell people that they need to change (repent). Isaiah had to walk around naked (Isaiah 20) for 3 years to deliver a message from God. Think he had many friends?? Ezekiel had to lay on his side (left and right for different prophecies) for a total of 430 days, in order to deliver a message from God! AND, during that time, he had to cook his food over ox dung! Wonder what his friends thought about him? He probably didn't have a ton of people wanting to have dinner with him! John the Baptist wore a camel's hide for clothing, ate locusts and honey, and was beheaded for his warnings. Ready to go hang out with him?

Do you get my point? When God used a man to prophecy in the bible, it didn't feel good most of the time. It wasn't a "feel good" message from the prophet. The prophet often had to suffer to deliver the message.

Is this good or bad fruit?

To fully make this point, I want to give you an example of a false prophet in 2020. I didn't call him a false prophet. He called himself one. I will not give his name here, nor am I trying to be political. It's just an example.

This man had quickly risen among the prophetic "circles", becoming a well-known prophet in America. His messages were full of elaborate dreams and visions of what God was showing him. He predicted revival in America (which did not happen), and he predicted the makeup of the Supreme Court changing (which did happen). It's hard to define "revival", so no one challenged him there. He predicted many things that would make a conservative Christian feel really good about the future being restored to good wholesome, Christian values. Who wouldn't want that to happen in America?? He created quite a following.

He predicted through a dream that Donald Trump would be re-elected President in 2020. He had a dream. Trump was stumbling. It looked like he didn't win, but he would be put into office as the winner. This sounded good to his base of followers. Here's the problem. It never happened. He gave specific dates that came and went...never happened. He's a false prophet, right? By definition, he has just proven himself to be a false prophet.

I'm going to throw you a "curveball" in the story. I will judge him, but remember, judgement can be positive! Once his prophecy did not come true, he went public with this statement: "I was wrong. I am deeply sorry, and I ask for your forgiveness. I would like to repent for inaccurately prophesying that Donald Trump would win a second term as the President of the United States."

I am actually going to defend this man. He did what Jesus asks us to do here in the Sermon on the Mount! He judged himself. He searched himself. He saw that he was wrong. He admitted it, repented, and asked for forgiveness! This is GOOD FRUIT!

He publicly admitted this, publicly asked for forgiveness, and took a break from ministry while he searched for how he was misled. He had to do some "soul searching". To me, it's BEAUTIFUL to see him do this. I don't want to see a man lose his following or ministry, but he is living out the words and instructions of Jesus!

At the time of this writing, he has now come back into ministry as a more humble servant of Jesus. I am judging him. I am saying that he did a good thing. It started out bad, but he changed!!! No one called him out about his false prophecy. He called himself out! Unfortunately, you don't see this often in ministry. When a pastor or evangelist or prophet is not living out the word of God and is confronted, it usually ends much worse in scandal, defiance, denial, and/or pride. But this man self-reflected, repented, stepped down to seek God more clearly, and asked for forgiveness.

Here's the problem. Who turned on him the hardest? Christians turned on him for being biblical. He received multiple death threats and thousands of emails from "Christ followers", saying very nasty and vulgar things to him, to his ministry, and to his family. He lost funding from donors who accused him of being a coward, a sellout, and a traitor to the Holy Spirit.

He actually listened to the Holy Spirit, followed the instructions Jesus gave in scripture, repented – and his followers turned on him HARSHLY. They would rather follow a false prophet than a repentant man of Jesus. Is it possible that his followers that turned on him represent the 5 bridesmaids that weren't prepared for the wedding feast? Is it possible that his followers are following a wider highway to hell, but are misled to think they are destined for heaven? That is between each of them and God, but I can say this. This prophet ended up showing good fruit. His followers that turned on him for repenting – they showed bad fruit.

This, unfortunately is the state or condition of many churches in America. We'd rather hear a "feel good" message or prophecy than hear a message that says we need to self-evaluate and change. We'd rather follow a false prophet or false teacher instead of a person that is willing to give up everything and all popularity to follow Jesus!

Ready for a true prophecy???

We are warned about this in scripture. Remember, a prophecy is a warning, based on God's word. Paul warned Timothy about the coming days we are seeing now. In 2 Timothy 3 verses 1-5, Paul says:

"You should know this, Timothy, that in the last days there will be very difficult times. ² For people will love only themselves and their money. They will be boastful and proud, scoffing at God, disobedient to their parents, and ungrateful. They will consider nothing sacred. ³ They will be unloving and unforgiving; they will slander others and have no self-control. They will be cruel and hate what is good. ⁴ They will betray their friends, be reckless, be puffed up with pride, and love pleasure rather than God. ⁵ They will act religious, but they will reject the power that could make them godly. Stay away from people like that!"

When we look at the state of our world, are we not living in a time where these scriptures are being lived out? Each one of these actually defines where we are as a culture today.

Now, let's look at what Paul tells Timothy in the next chapter. 2 Timothy 4, verses 1-4 says:

"I solemnly urge you in the presence of God and Christ Jesus, who will someday judge the living and the dead when he comes to set up his Kingdom: ² Preach the word of God. Be prepared, whether the time is favorable or not. Patiently correct, rebuke, and encourage your people with good teaching.

³ For a time is coming when people will no longer listen to sound and wholesome teaching. They will follow their own desires and will look for teachers who will tell them whatever their itching ears want to hear. ⁴ They will reject the truth and chase after myths."

When we look at the state of our churches in America, are we not living in a time where these scriptures are being lived out? People would rather hear a false prophecy about good things than to hear a true prophecy from Paul that things are about to get really difficult. Paul gives a few clues of what the last days will look like, and we are seeing ALL of these things happen in our society and in our churches.

Please don't get wrapped up in doom and gloom and miss what Paul says though. He says keeping preaching the word of God! Be prepared! He says whether the time is favorable or not – be prepared. And – patiently correct, rebuke, and encourage your people with good teaching.

That's my goal. I'm not claiming to be a prophet. I do have the common sense to see the state of our world, as well as state of our churches/teachers/prophets. Whether we are in the end or not is up to God, not me. All I can do is preach the word of God, and be prepared, and help prepare you. Whether the time is favorable or not, preach the word – PATIENTLY correcting…Patiently rebuking… and ENCOURAGING you with good teaching.

I consider this good teaching to teach you what it means to be known by Jesus. I consider this good teaching to teach you how to reach the narrow gate. I consider this good teaching to teach you how to avoid false prophets.

Whether we are in the "end times" or not, I don't have the answer about the when the final day is. However, I do know that none of us are promised tomorrow. We need to be ready to meet Jesus NOW! Be prepared!

Questions and Application for Chapter 16
1. Do you treat others the way you want to be treated, no matter how they have treated you?
2. As we process through the Sermon on the Mount, are you making changes in your thoughts (your heart)? Are those changes leading to positive changes in your actions?
3. Are you confident that you'll enter the narrow gate? That you'll be one of the "5"? If not, what is the biggest area that you need to work on to achieve this?
4. Is there a false prophet or false teacher that you follow? If yes, will you simply stop listening to them?
5. Are you prepared to meet Jesus today? (Be careful that rejection or satan's lies don't influence your answer…)
6. Challenge – Think about how you treat those you come in contact with today (and each day). Treat them the way you want to be treated, and see how that changes your mood. If you are following a false prophet or teacher, STOP!

Prayer
"Father, please help me to treat everyone the way I would want to be treated, no matter how they treat me. Help me to understand that this doesn't mean that I become a 'door mat' for people. Help me to know who I need to get away from, due to how they treat me. Please help expose false prophets and false teachers to me, so that I can get away from them! Please protect me from the wolves! Father, please show me what I need to work on today to be prepared to meet Jesus on that day that He returns. I bind up any and all fear in Jesus's name that is associated with the thought of His return! Come LORD Jesus come!"

17

The grand finale!

The big verse!
We finally made it to the verse that drove my desire and calling to write this book – Matthew 7 verses 21-23:

²¹ "Not everyone who calls out to me, 'Lord! Lord!' will enter the Kingdom of Heaven. Only those who actually do the will of my Father in heaven will enter. ²² On judgment day many will say to me, 'Lord! Lord! We prophesied in your name and cast out demons in your name and performed many miracles in your name.' ²³ But I will reply, 'I never knew you. Get away from me, you who break God's laws.'

How many of you started reading this book, hoping that I would provide you a checklist of what you need to do to be known by Jesus? As Christians, we sometimes get lulled into trying to check off things on the important "Jesus list", if we are honest with ourselves.

Here's the beauty. Jesus did give us a checklist. I've done my best to explain His checklist. But, it's not about checking things off the list. It's about allowing these things to change who you are, or who you will be. Jesus's grace covers our past (and future) sins, but He has been very clear that He expects us to change how we think. He expects us to change how we act. He expects our actions to line up with the heart change, and not be a fake action that looks holy when it's not.

Jesus says here very clearly that not everyone that calls out to Him as "Lord, Lord" will enter the kingdom of heaven. He says that some will do some incredible things in His name, but He will not know them. "We prophesied in your name"...."We cast out demons in your name"..."We performed many miracles in your name"...yet, He still doesn't know them.

Let's be careful not to get wrapped up in a fear or a worry about not being known, and miss what He says here. ONLY THOSE WHO ACTUALLY DO THE WILL OF MY FATHER IN HEAVEN WILL ENTER. THOSE WHO BREAK GOD'S LAWS WILL NOT BE KNOWN.

It's not enough to know Jesus. Demons know Him. You have to do what you are taught in scripture to be known by Jesus. He says "only those who ACTUALLY DO the will of My Father...". He's just laid out the will of His Father by fully explaining and preaching up what the Law (the instructions) are about. Now, He says DO what He says, and don't break God's instructions.

Do you understand now why I painstakingly went through the explanation of the "Law" in Chapter 6? If we don't understand Chapter 6 completely, we stand in risk of violating the ONE thing that Jesus says makes us known by Him.

To the super religious that will only read the King James version of the bible, it says "depart from me, ye that work iniquity". Want the true Hebrew translation here? "Those who break God's laws" or "ye that work ininquity" means someone who is Lawless due to a corrupt heart.

This entire sermon has been about heart change and making sure our hearts are being molded into what God wants versus what the world wants. These people that would do miracles, healings, and prophecies in Jesus name that are referenced in verse 22, were or are using Jesus with the wrong heart for their personal gain. It was happening then, and it is still happening today. People in churches all over America, or people on social media ministry platforms will use Jesus for personal gain. That's a lawless heart – that's a corrupt heart.

To be known by Jesus is actually very easy in principle – allow Him access to the dark places of your heart, and actively work to change those areas to line up with His thoughts and desires versus lining up with the selfish, sinful desires that come so easy for us. Easy in principle, but hard to walk out at times due to how powerful the lure of sin is.

For some, this is an easy transition because they are so sick of their sinful nature. That was me. I'm not saying that the road to this point has not been hard. It has been. I'm not saying I don't have more room to grow. I will be learning the heart of the Father and hopefully changing my heart to His till the day I die. This journey is not about perfection or works, it's about heart change. It's about allowing the Father to change your sinful worldly passions and thoughts to what He wants – His Will. It's about allowing those new thoughts to produce new actions that produce good fruit. It's about relying on the grace of Jesus when you fail, which will happen because we are still human. It's about relying on the grace of Jesus when you take a step back – so that you can take 2 or more steps forward!

The sinner's prayer…

I am about to make a statement that might make you scratch your head – until I fully explain it. I am concerned that the "sinner's prayer" is sending many people straight down the highway to hell.

Often, we tell the story of Jesus – death, burial, resurrection – all for the salvation of sins and to allow us to be reunified with the Father in eternity. All that is good! So far so good. Then, we say "all you have to do is say this prayer with me to secure your eternal life". We walk people through a prayer to "ask Jesus" into their hearts. They say the prayer, and we rejoice. We say things like angels are rejoicing. We should rejoice when someone makes a decision to follow Jesus! Angels are rejoicing when someone makes a decision to follow Jesus!

Here's the problem. If we tell them that "all they have to do" is say that prayer, we leave out this whole verse where Jesus says you have to actually DO what His instructions say. You have to change your heart not to be lawless.

Now, maybe you say the "sinner's prayer" and a true miracle happens. Your heart is changed in an instant and you begin to obey Christ. I hope that has happened for you and for others. God can do what He wants and make it that easy and straight forward. That's not where I'm going with this.

Maybe that prayer is a great place to start. What's next? Jesus said "Make disciples". He never said make "Believers". He says that we are to "make disciples". As we mentioned at the beginning, even the demons believe in Jesus AND they tremble.

So, what does it mean to become a disciple? It means to begin to read your bible, for example, and begin to change your thoughts and actions to line up with what God wants and instructs. Let's say that I say the "sinner's prayer", and I feel like I'm all good and saved now. If no one then teaches me that I'm not supposed to chase the world's success, where is the heart change? If no one then teaches me that I'm supposed to work on my anger because it's like murder, where is the heart change? If no one then teaches me that I'm supposed to stop lusting after women outside of my marriage, where is the heart change? If no one teaches me that revenge is not good, where is my heart change? If no one teaches me to love those that are hardest to love (my enemies), where is my heart change? If no one teaches me about good works, proper giving, or how to pray, where is my heart change? I'm simply walking through the Sermon on the Mount with these examples and these questions.

The sinner's prayer may radically change your heart, but my concern is for the 1,000's that say it weekly at church, but have zero heart change. I worked at a church. Let's say there were 1,200 people per week attending. At the end of each message, the pastor would ask people if they wanted to be saved by raising their hand. Here's what I noticed. Each week, some of the same people were continually raising their hands. I started asking them why? It was loving...I was not accusatory. I might say, "I've noticed that you raised your hand 3 weeks in a row about giving your life to Jesus. Are you concerned that you haven't?" Time after time, the answer was "I want to give my life to Jesus, but I really don't know what that means or if I have."

I'm not trying to be critical of the pastor for asking the question. I'm trying to point out a major problem in our churches today. If we tell someone to just believe or to just say a prayer, and we don't teach them about the heart change piece that produces action change and life change – then, we are guilty, by definition, of being false teachers!

In John 14:15, Jesus says "If you love me, obey my commandments." That word commandment literally refers back to the "Mosaic Law". Again, this is why Chapter 6 of this book is so important for us to grasp!

In John 3:36, Jesus says "And anyone who believes in God's Son has eternal life. Anyone who doesn't obey the Son will never experience eternal life but remains under God's angry judgment."

Did you catch that? It says anyone who "believes" in God's Son has eternal life. Then, it says anyone who does not "obey" the Son will NEVER experience eternal life. If you only read the first statement, all you have to do is believe. If you read both statements, you learn that to truly believe means that you obey. So, yes, all you have to do is believe in Jesus to receive eternal life. That's a fact. But, we have to know that true belief means that we obey. Each time that Paul tells us in scripture that we are saved when we "believe", we need to understand those words to say when we believed and obeyed.

Many translations goof this up. The King James says:

"He that believeth on the Son hath everlasting life: and he that believeth not the Son shall not see life; but the wrath of God abideth on him."

Sounds straight forward, right? Believe in the Son = everlasting life (eternal life); Believeth not in the Son = no eternal life, but wrath.

Let's look at the NIV:

"Whoever believes in the Son has eternal life, but whoever rejects the Son will not see life, for God's wrath remains on them."

Believe in the Son = eternal life; Reject the Son = no eternal life.

Now, let's look at the Greek words used. I'll mix English in with the Greek to make this easier on us! It actually says: He that "pisteuo" (thinks to be true) in the Son has eternal life, but he that "apeitheo" (does not comply with) the Son does not have eternal life. The better translation of that verse is the NLT over the KJV or the NIV. This was not intended to be a lesson in translations, but I hope you see how CRITICAL this is to get correct.

If I read that as – believe and get eternal life; don't believe and don't get eternal life – then, all I have to do is think it to be true. I think it to be true that Jesus is the Messiah! However, if I read that more accurately from the Greek, I not only have to think it to be true, I have to comply with what the Son says. I have to do what He says. I have to obey Him.

Do you see what I mean about the sinner's prayer sending people to hell? If you read this and think that I'm being too religious, too law based, too "works" based, you can make your own determination on what's enough. All I know is that Jesus just said some heavy words in Matthew 7 that line up with what I just said. He said only those who DO the will of my Father will enter the Kingdom of Heaven. And He said that some people that "believed" in Him did some things in His name – some pretty awesome things in His name – and He still didn't know them because their hearts were not changed.

If we are living in the time that Paul warned Timothy about, we need to understand this and teach this correctly, before it's too late!

Final instructions...

Jesus finishes this sermon with verses 24-27, where He says:

[24] "Therefore everyone who hears these words of mine and puts them into practice is like a wise man who built his house on the rock. [25] The rain came down, the streams rose, and the winds blew and beat against that house; yet it did not fall, because it had its foundation on the rock. [26] But everyone who hears these words of mine and does not put them into practice is like a foolish man who built his house on sand. [27] The rain came down, the streams rose, and the winds blew and beat against that house, and it fell with a great crash."

Once again, Jesus says "do something". Everyone who hears these words of Mine and PUTS THEM INTO PRACTICE…..is like a wise man that built his house on a solid foundation. A solid foundation allows you to withstand the storms. A weak foundation (believing but not obeying) falls.

Jesus is the ROCK – He is the cornerstone of the church. If you build your foundation on Him by believing and obeying – by believing and putting His words into practice – you will be able to withstand the storms till you meet Him in Paradise. If you read this and do nothing with it, you are a foolish person who will not withstand the storms. His words…not mine. I didn't call you foolish if you don't obey Jesus. Jesus did!

The world has a low standard of obedience. Unfortunately, the church is lowering it's standard every day, while still using the name of Jesus as they do it. Jesus has spent this entire Sermon on the Mount warning us to raise our standard to His, not lower our standard to the world's. Raising your standard of obedience is what gets you known by Jesus!

Jesus's grace is there when you fail – while you are trying to raise your standard of obedience. Jesus's grace is there when you stumble – while you are trying to raise your standard of obedience. Jesus's grace is there when you don't measure up – while you are trying to raise your standard. Jesus's grace is there to show you when, where, and how you need to change (repent) – while you are trying to raise your standard.

Come to Him broken, hurting, as a failure, but don't use His Grace to stay broken. This is not about perfection, it's about heart change...it's about trying. The more you try, the more obedient you will be. The more you get to know Jesus and His instructions, the more you will want obey Him. The more you obey Him, the more He knows you!

As we end, I can't tell you if you'll be known by Jesus or not. Only you can answer that question.

WILL JESUS KNOW YOU?

Final Q&A
1. After reading this and after studying Jesus's Sermon on the Mount, do you feel like you know Jesus better?
2. Do you feel like He knows you better?
3. What is one thing (or multiple things) that you need to work on to be better known by Jesus?
4. As you read this book, is there an area that you feel like you're doing really good? – an area where you feel confident that Jesus knows you?
5. Do you have more hope and peace after studying this topic?
6. Challenge – Go back and review the chapters where you need to improve. At the same time, give yourself credit in the areas where you are excelling! Pick one place and begin to make the changes that you need to make to be better known by Jesus! Take one step at a time and get to know Jesus!

Prayer
"Father, Thank you that your Son Jesus died for us! Thank you that your Son Jesus gave us this blueprint so that we can be assured that we are known by You! Father, if there is an area or areas that I need to work on, please show me those so that I can work on those things. If there is an area that I'm doing well in, please show me that so that I can be encouraged. Father, please help me to know the difference between your Holy Spirit conviction versus a lie from the enemy. Please give me discernment to know the difference. Father, I know you! And I'm thankful that you know me!!"

www.ingramcontent.com/pod-product-compliance
Lightning Source LLC
Chambersburg PA
CBHW030656060526
44119CB00097B/462/J